D0826614

Pack
Your
Own
Parachute

How to Survive Mergers, Takeovers, and Other Corporate Disasters

By Paul Hirsch

Addison-Wesley Publishing Company, Inc.
Reading, Massachusetts
Menlo Park, California
New York • Don Mills, Ontario
Wokingham, England
Amsterdam • Bonn • Sydney
Singapore • Tokyo • Madrid
Bogotá • Santiago • San Juan

The author gratefully acknowledges permission to reprint materials supplied by the following sources:

Page 11: From Laurie Cohen and Jonathan Dahl, "Phillips is Pressured by Debt, Oil-Price Slide." Reprinted by permission of the *Wall Street Journal*, © Dow Jones & Company, Inc. (1985). All rights reserved.

Page 19: Mike Luckovich cartoon reprinted by permission of Copley News Service.

Page 27: From J. W. Lorsch, "In Defense of the Corporate Defender." Copyright © 1984 by the New York Times Company. Reprinted by permission.

Pages 30, 62, 80, 140: From Myron Magnet, "Help! My Company Has Just Been Taken Over," *Fortune*. © 1984 Time Inc. All rights reserved.

Pages 30, 71, 75, 95, 98–100: From Felix Kessler, "Managers Without a Company," *Fortune*. © Time Inc. All rights reserved.

Continued on next page

Library of Congress Cataloging-in-Publication Data

Hirsch, Paul Morris.
Pack your own parachute.

Includes index.
1. Executives — United States — Dismissal of.
2. Consolidation and merger of corporations — United States. 3. Corporate culture — United States. I. Title.
HD38.25.U6H578 1987 658.4'09 87–14388
ISBN 0–201–12205–7

Cover design by Steve Snider
Text design by Outside Designs
Set in 9.5-point Palatino by Neil W. Kelley, Georgetown, MA

ABCDEFGHIJ-DO-8987
First printing, September 1987

Pages 32–33: From Paul Hirsch, "From Ambushes to Golden Parachutes," *American Journal of Sociology*. © 1986. Reprinted by permission of the University of Chicago.

Pages 43– 44: "Tale of Survival in the Takeover Jungle," reprinted by permission of Art Buchwald. © Art Buchwald.

Pages 55–56: From Ken Wells and Carol Hymowitz, "Takeover Trauma: Gulf's Managers Find Merger Into Chevron Forces Many Changes." Reprinted by permission of the *Wall Street Journal*. © Dow Jones & Company, Inc. (1984). All rights reserved.

Page 57: Cartoon reprinted by permission of Richard Orlin. © 1985.

Page 71: From *Death of a Salesman* by Arthur Miller. Copyright 1949, Renewed © 1977 by Arthur Miller. Reprinted by permission of Viking-Penguin Inc.

Pages 76–79: From *Not Working: An Oral History of the Unemployed* by Harry Maurer. Copyright © 1979 by Harry Maurer. Reprinted by permission of Henry Holt and Company.

Pages 82–85: From *Termination: The Closing at Baker Plant* by Alfred Slote. Published 1969 by Bobbs-Merrill Co.; reissued 1977 by the Institute for Social Research, University of Michigan. Reprinted by permission of Alfred Slote.

Pages 96, 101: From Thomas O'Boyle, "Loyalty Ebbs at Many Companies as Employees Grow Disillusioned." Reprinted by permission of the *Wall Street Journal*. © Dow Jones & Company, Inc. (1985). All rights reserved.

Contents

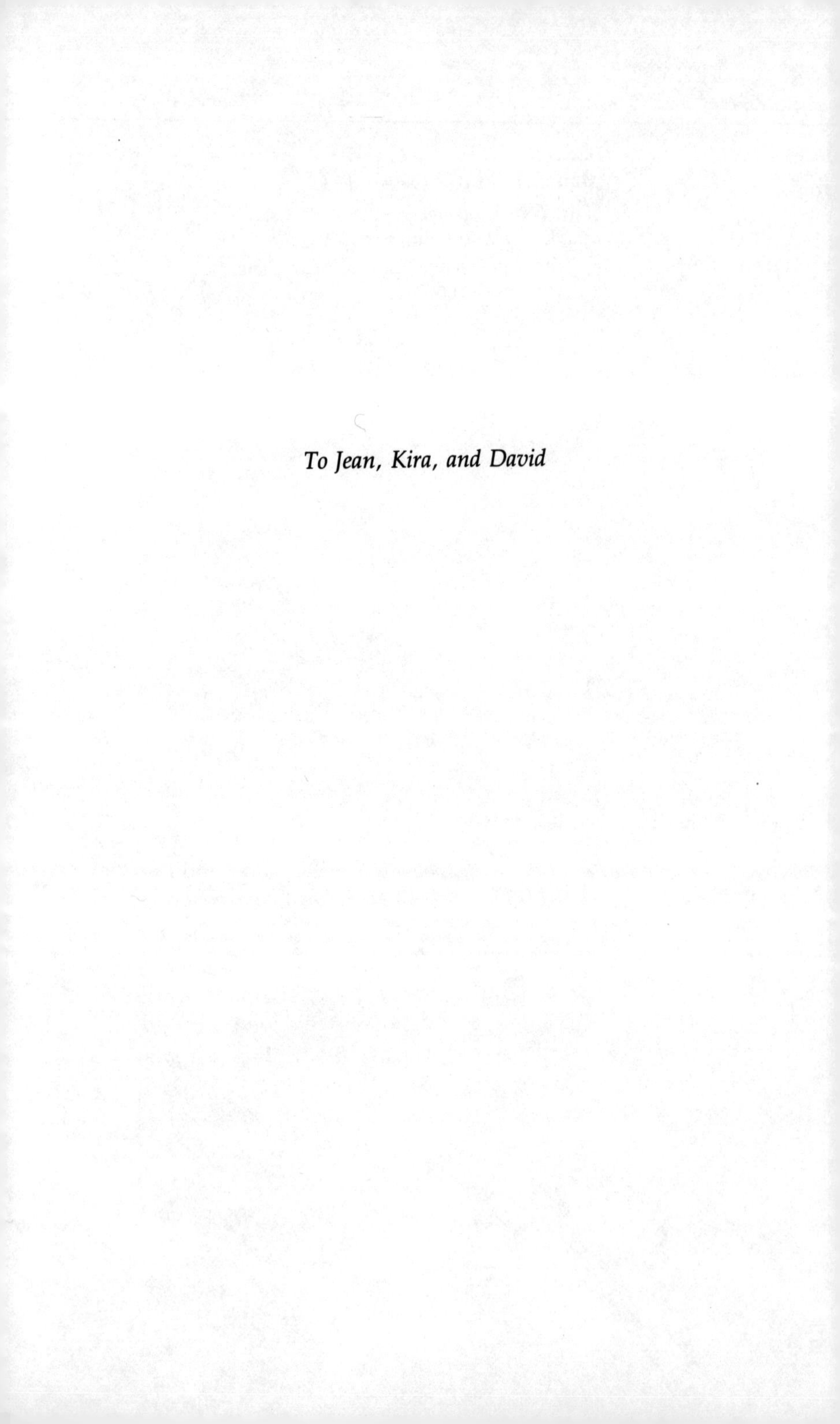

To Jean, Kira, and David

Preface

In 1978, Professor Thomas Whisler and I received a research grant from the National Science Foundation to examine the changing world of Fortune 500 directors. At the time, big corporations had just responded to public pressure by expanding their boards to include more women, minority group members, and nonbusinessmen. In another break with tradition, United Auto Workers' President Douglas Fraser had just won and accepted a seat on Chrysler's board. We expected chief executives and traditional board members to resent the arrival of so many "outsiders" in their hallowed chambers. But these social issues were hardly on their minds. Instead, our study turned up something far more surprising, important, and increasingly ominous in the years that followed.

Repeatedly we heard directors express anger, fear, and contempt for Wall Street investment bankers, a group of former friends no longer welcome in most corporate boardrooms. With absolute unanimity, even back in the late 1970s, more than fifty Fortune 500 directors and chief executives described Wall Street's bankers as a new enemy force engineering takeovers and downsizings, and creating dangerously high levels of corporate debt.

The big news was that directors were starting to worry about the very survival of the corporation as they knew it. The financial hailstorm they saw coming was serious and fundamental. It was also very human and, at root, bound up with broader issues concerning our society's attitudes toward fairness in work and employment. Our directors foresaw, but could not imagine the extent of, the economic and psychological pain these wrenching changes would soon force on American managers. The coming wave of forced mergers, takeovers, and restructurings was only just beginning.

The vehemence of these directors' comments about their shattered bonds of trust with Wall Street bankers was very hard to forget. It came back repeatedly with every headline about another battle for control of a major U.S. corporation and whenever a major company announced management cutbacks along with plans to buy back its own stock. To appease Wall Street's mounting pressure for higher and higher short-term earnings, our biggest and best-known corporations also began cutting payrolls and forcing out talented managers.

As a professor of management concerned with the health and vitality of corporate cultures, I watched these developments with mounting concern. The serious human resource implications were unmistakable, as managers' lives were shattered by the waves of firings, layoffs, and forced early retirements in companies targeted by this near-total fixation on short-run profits, finance, and share price. Managers were surely headed for a serious fall.

Throughout the early 1980s, there was remarkably little public discussion of this serious problem. To be sure, the drama and suspense of corporate takeovers captured the imagination of millions, but the focus remained almost entirely in the financial arena. Few questions arose about who was minding the store while all this was going on, or how the target firm's managers and employees would react and be treated after the dust settled and the deals were cut.

In the summer of 1984, I was asked to speak on the "Managerial Implications of Corporate Takeovers" before a gathering of alumni from the University of Chicago's Graduate School of Business. As we assembled in a meeting room at the First National Bank's building, I saw many former students who had graduated into good jobs, as well as other alums with whom I was less familiar. In my talk, I suggested the era of good companies looking out for their managers was ending. I proposed that before long, it would be important and necessary to think more like "free agents" without a reserve clause—that for better or worse, since the caring corporate employer was becoming an endangered species, managers would have to exercise more independence, consider alternative opportunities on a regular basis, and look out more for themselves.

When I finished speaking, there was absolute silence in the room. Maybe my topic was totally off the mark. I looked around, hoping someone would break the spell. They all seemed involved in their own private thoughts. After a few superficial, polite questions, the meeting ended. Immediately, people lined up to talk in a more private setting. It suddenly became clear that what I was warning managers to beware of had recently happened to many sitting in that same room. Former students I have known over the years all asked how was I so familiar with what they thought was just their own private hell.

These managers were in deep shock. That summer, some of them had just gone through exactly what I was talking about.

Major Chicago corporations were being thrashed by takeovers and restructurings. After its own takeover of conglomerate Norton Simon, the Esmark Corporation, earlier known as Swift Meats, was taken over by the Beatrice Foods Company. Got that? Beatrice, in turn, was rumored to be taking on such enormous debt so it would be a less attractive takeover target to Nestlé, which went out and bought Carnation Company instead. Running these businesses now meant deciding which jobs and business units would disappear next in order to pay for all these financial and ownership fireworks. During that same summer, Montgomery Ward was being downsized by Mobil, which had done miserably with it ever since engineering its takeover twelve years earlier. Northwest Industries' new owner, William Farley, had just announced that much of its staff would soon be fired. Masonite was disappearing as an independent corporation, and Jewel Food Stores' board had just reluctantly endorsed a hostile bid for that company.

My audience was clearly upset over how to respond to the managerial chaos imposed by downsizings and takeovers. My lecture had touched a nerve, and things were even worse than I had thought. After all, these managers were among the best and brightest MBAs in the country, and if they were already feeling scared and vulnerable, one had to wonder how this craziness must be affecting the rest of America's managers.

As word of my interest and concern got around, I located more and more middle managers interested in talking about how their careers and companies were so rapidly changing. I interviewed more than seventy-five people, representing a variety of industries and age groups across the country. Some welcomed the new opportunities for advancement in restructured companies. More complained that there were now fewer positions to advance into at their firms. Most striking was that everybody by now knew someone caught by surprise when his or her company responded to pressures for downsizing, divestments, and other preventative measures to avoid takeover. But despite seeing people get hurt all around them, these managers nearly all believed it simply wouldn't happen to them. But today, as companies downsize, "demass," and "flatten their hierarchies," can employees afford any longer to place all of their trust in a single employer?

I posed this question to management experts Allan Cox, author of *Inside Corporate America* and *Confessions of a Corporate Headhunter*, and Russell Roberts, managing principal at human resource consultants Sibson & Company, at the University of Chicago's annual management conference in April 1985. Both stated the growing consensus that neither employees nor companies should any longer assume managers will have a full career at just one company. Rather, both parties should always keep an eye on their current needs, and on how much the other is contributing to meet them. Free agents should always know their alternatives.

After chairing this panel, entitled "Is Company Loyalty Going Out of Style?," I decided to write this book. Managers need a better handle on how to respond in this far colder and more calculating business climate. When major corporations are crippled so professional stock speculators can put another notch on their belt, much more has occurred than the elimination of "waste" and "fat" in the human form of employees and corporate managers. The very long-term growth, quality of work life, and, yes, even the soul of these companies have been sold out for a few dollars more.

It is important for the managers who run our most important companies, and for society, to realize that these are controversial power grabs that do not have or deserve everyone's approval and support. It is also high time to point out how deceptive and insulting the slick, self-serving rhetoric of corporate raiders and their financial allies has become. The new generation of button-down Wall Street hitmen needs to join plain-speaking raiders James "I do it to make money" Goldsmith, Carl ". . . My first motive is to make money" Icahn, Irwin "My . . . objective is to make money" Jacobs, and ex-arbitrageur Ivan "My master is my purse" Boesky in acknowledging greed as their main motive. To frame the brutal and unplanned restructurings which corporate raids dictate as a public service is a gross overstatement, distracting needed attention from the harm and human cost these exploits in financial brinksmanship leave in their wake.

Corporations' incapacity to take care of their own managers has serious implications for managers' careers. Wherever companies trade off future positions and lines of business to borrow and distribute immediate cash on the barrel, the quality of work life will deteriorate. There cannot be as much room for attractive promotions in companies shrinking in size and unable to take risks on attractive new products because they are paying off enormous debt loads.

In this new environment, managers must better protect themselves and act like free agents. In today's job world the best defense is a good offense. But taking the initiative to become truly alert to new opportunities requires understanding that you really cannot rely on your company to look out for you. If you are a manager, you must learn how to pack your own parachute.

Acknowledgments

This book could not have been written without the help of many managers, research assistants, colleagues, students, a wonderful secretary, and other friends. I wish to thank, first, the many dedicated managers who spoke so honestly and freely. They must remain anonymous because their interviews were given in confidence.

The superb research assistance and clear thinking of Wendy Espeland and David Wilford added ideas and depth at every step along the way. Espeland and Wilford are superb organizers and interviewers. David Wilford also wrote the initial drafts for chapters 4 and 5. Dennis Wheaton filed eye-opening reports from Bartlesville, Oklahoma. David Patten critically examined the arguments most often made for hostile takeovers. And John Andrews organized the Glossary of Merger and Takeover Terminology.

Professors at business schools across America were consistently generous with their time, ideas, and support. At the University of Chicago Graduate School of Business, I am especially indebted to my colleagues John Gallagher, Jack Gould, Robert Graves, John Jeuck, Richard Thain, and Thomas Whisler. Among the many I wish to thank at other universities are Janice Beyer, Nicole Biggart, Tom Cummings, Robert Eccles, Rick Gilkey, Leonard Greenhalgh, Larry Greiner, JoAnn Martin, Philip Mirvis, Horace Newcomb, William Ouchi, Jonathan Rieder, Robert Sutton, Andrew Van de Ven, Karl Weick, Harrison White, and Mayer Zald.

Current and former students also have been consistently helpful. From Chicago to Singapore, they have won and lost in role-plays of mergers and acquisitions, and then effectively argued with each other, and with me, over what is fair and who comes out ahead. Among those who have stayed in touch, and to whom I owe a special debt, are Chia Hock Hwa, Alexander Lourie, Lincoln Kaye, and Sara Newman.

Of the many superb journalists covering business, five writers I wish to single out for their early and outstanding coverage of issues taken up here are Isadore Barmash, Walter Kiechel III, Myron Magnet, Tim Metz, and Allan Sloan.

George Gibson and Martha Moutray, my editors at Addison-Wesley, have been enormously helpful and patient, as has my agent, John Wright. Elizabeth Ebert, Dan Frank, and Tom Panelas have also read single chapters and helped to improve them.

Over the last decade, Evelyn Shropshire has unraveled and typed much of my writing with constant dedication and good humor. This book is no exception and I am grateful for her help. Peg Wiedemann and Jane Ann Layton have also contributed their excellent secretarial skills. Other friends who have helped with this book in their own way include Linda Forgeron, Alice and

Henry Hirsch, Kathryn and Leonard Klue, Edward Laumann, and Stuart Michaels.

I thank them all. And for constant support and companionship, especially, thank you, Jean.

Pack
Your
Own
Parachute

Introduction: Oklahoma Meets Wall Street

"We're still in business," said spokesman Steve Milburn. He said despite the fact that the company has shut down its famous oil well on the state capital grounds in Oklahoma City, along with its historic Burbank Field wells in Osage county, Phillips still has 8,000 producing wells in the U.S.

Bartlesville Examiner-Enterprise
August 1986

Phillips Petroleum was on the ropes. The giant oil company dropped nearly 10,000 people between 1985 and 1987, close to 25 percent of its work force worldwide. Bartlesville, Oklahoma, its affluent, largely white-collar headquarters city of 38,000, was especially hard hit.

"Anyone with the brains God gave a grasshopper is not buying a house in Bartlesville," said one Phillips manager in summer 1986. Two of the only retailers with something to smile about were the local U-Haul and Ryder truck renters, whose volume always goes up "as people pack up to move on . . . 'If you wanted a truck today, you couldn't get one,'" said Gordon Brown, owner of Bartlesville Auto Supply. Social workers noticed a different kind of increase—in the amount of anxiety and tension among

Phillips employees as they saw their job prospects dwindling. Even before the waves of layoffs and early retirements, Jerry Poppenhouse, art director at Phillips, told a reporter, "The mood now is, 'Who's going to be next?'" Another manager and Bartlesville resident added, "Outsiders don't understand that even if you aren't laid off, or your co-workers aren't, you still go to church or scouts or soccer with someone who is."

Phillips Petroleum, the nation's seventeenth largest industrial corporation and eighth biggest oil producer, was cash poor. Deeply in debt, it had to raise vast sums of money very quickly. Asked which of the company's far-flung operations might be for sale in 1985, Chairman and Chief Executive Officer William Douce said, "All of them—and that's no joke." This included oil fields in Africa, Alaska, the Gulf of Mexico, and the North Sea around Holland—where Phillips had been the first to discover oil that helped Europe become less dependent on supplies from the Middle East. All or parts of these were soon sold, along with coal and geothermal facilities in Texas, Utah, Nevada, and California. In addition to selling off petroleum reserves and other properties, Phillips axed or delayed some big research and exploration projects.

Cutting back its work force and payroll was another policy Phillips adopted to raise cash. Nearly every employee was offered incentives to quit voluntarily before the company moved on to layoffs and terminations. People fifty-five or older were promised a larger pension if they signed up for early retirement immediately. A majority of long-service managers at all levels took the offer. Some were ready and welcomed the opportunity. But others felt rejected, helpless, and all alone.

"Some simply have resigned themselves to resigning," said one. "I mean to retiring without knowing if they would be able to get another job and if they will need one . . . Many would rather still be working, and not only just for the money." Another recent retiree added:

> The ones I feel sorry for are those still in their middle fifties. Fifty-five is early to retire. There's no other work here right now, though if you want to go to California or New York you can probably start over. But it's not just a matter of getting in your car and going. Say you're a homeowner. If you were transferred the company would take it off your hands. But you're retired now. You have this real estate you can't dispose of. Right now I don't think you can even rent out many of the houses for sale. It's a tough situation.

In spite of these hardships, Phillips employees and Bartlesville residents still considered themselves "lucky." Only seventeen months earlier, Phillips had won a crucial victory for them. It succeeded, against strong odds, in keeping the company independent and in Oklahoma. In an extraordinary four-month period etched in the memory of Bartlesville's small population, corporate raiders T. Boone Pickens and Carl Icahn each attempted to purchase Phillips Petroleum from its shareholders. "How would you feel," asked one Bartlesville citizen, "if Godzilla and Frankenstein both stomped through your town?"

To beat them back, Phillips had repurchased much of its own stock and taken on billions of dollars in new debt to pay for it. Both current and former employees knew why the company had to raise so much cash. They knew their pain stemmed from the bills falling due for this victory. If employment was down here, many said, look at what happened to people at the other companies that tangled with T. Boone Pickens or blew themselves up to avoid him.

"Look at Gulf and its white knight, Chevron," exclaimed one Phillips staffer. "I have a good friend at Chevron. In another year or two they'll be operating both companies with the same number of employees Chevron had when they took Gulf over. That's 50 percent fewer people working than when the two companies were running separately." Before driving Gulf into Chevron's embrace, Pickens had made profitable runs on Cities Service (in neighboring Tulsa), Superior Oil, Supron Energy, and General American Oil (which chose to be acquired by Phillips in 1983, rather than be taken over by Pickens's Mesa Petroleum Company). None of these companies exists independently any longer. "The other companies all lost their identities, and we feared that," commented another Phillips veteran. "Everybody's pleased Phillips was able to retain it. We're grateful the company is still intact."

Soon after Phillips repulsed its invaders, one of its computer engineers, A. J. Lafaro, received an unusual request from Los Angeles, home of Unocal ("76") Oil. Pickens had selected Unocal as his next takeover target, and some of its employees remembered a "Boonebuster" T-shirt worn all over Bartlesville during the time Phillips was fighting the same battle. Lafaro had designed it at about the same time that the movie *Ghostbusters* was a big success. He superimposed the international symbol for "No" over a picture of Mr. Pickens, who also purchased some to give as Christmas presents. Unocal employees now wanted them for their impending struggle. Said one Phillips official, "Believe me, if they're going through anything like what we went through, they could use [them]!"

The "Boonebuster" shirt is only one example of the enthusiasm and commitment Bartlesville citizens showed for Phillips during its bitter fights to stay independent. The community was shocked, angered, and scared at the possibility of losing any or all of the company to a corporate takeover. Here was the largest employer in the state brought to its knees, with its fate hinging on maneuvers in far-away boardrooms on Wall Street. "I get the feeling that a bunch of strangers are out there playing Russian roulette with the future of this community—this state, really—and I don't like it," said Josef Derryberry, a jeweler in Bartlesville.

At a crisis forum of 8,000 residents, speakers discussing what the loss of Phillips would mean to the community and nation included the area's school superintendent, the director of the

National Institute for Petroleum and Energy Research, the Sears manager at a newly built shopping mall, a former vice president of what had been the Cities Service Oil Company, student officers from the local high school, and the Osage Indian chief on whose nearby land Frank Phillips had originally struck oil. Rudy Taylor, a newspaper publisher in neighboring Caney, Kansas, received a standing ovation when he said:

> Without Phillips, we'd just be Mayberry R.F.D., and with Phillips we have a lot of confidence in our future and we have a world of ideas on how we can improve our little corner of the world . . . Our chief industry in Caney, Kansas, is Phillips Petroleum Company; it's been that way for over a half century and . . . because of their influence our community is a progressive one. We feel the Phillips influence in our schools, and in our places of business and in our churches and our lodges . . . We're in this fight with you and we're in it to win. Let's do it!"

Looking back on the community's outpouring of support, a Phillips manager later commented:

> Farming and oil are the lifeblood of this part of the country. And farming was already in bad shape. Bartlesville has no other appreciable industry that I am aware of. It's pretty much Phillips, and if Phillips goes or starts trimming down, everything turns down. The impact on the community if Phillips were to go is that others would just vanish. Bartlesville would be a ghost town. But as long as there is some nucleus of Phillips here, there will be the Phillips people and there will be these other people from the supporting communities in surrounding areas who will come to Bartlesville.

Christmas in Bartlesville, 1984, turned out to be a happy one. On Christmas eve, just three weeks after Pickens launched his takeover bid, he and Phillips announced a settlement. "We were very pleased Phillips maintained its identity," recalls one retiree, "but at the same time I think people resented Mr. Pickens making the profit he did." In financial terms, Phillips agreed to repurchase the 8.9 million shares in the company Pickens had accumulated, for $10 a share more than they had cost him. This yielded a gross profit of $89 million for Pickens on shares he had held for roughly six weeks. Phillips would also pay Pickens and his group $25 million more to cover expenses they ran up in making their run on the company.

But this was only the beginning. The settlement also required Phillips to present an expensive plan at its next annual meeting designed to raise its shares' value for other investors as well. The company would propose to buy back 38 percent of all its stock. (Pickens had only owned about 6 percent, or less than one-sixth of the additional amount the company agreed to repurchase.) To remove Pickens's takeover threat and satisfy his demands, Phillips had spent $57 million in three weeks and was now committed to borrowing nearly $3 *billion* to cover its proposed stock buyback program.

As the dust settled from one battle and the new year got under way, Phillips next heard from Carl Icahn, perhaps Wall Street's most feared financier and corporate raider. Icahn was buying big blocks of the company's stock and demanding Phillips pay more for the shares it proposed to buy back. He had substantial support from what *New York Times* writer Daniel Cuff called "those cold and distant institutions that own 47 percent of Phillips [stock] and hold the key to its future." On February 5, 1985, Icahn offered to buy Phillips from its shareholders for a higher price. Now in its second battle in two months, there was little doubt at Phillips or in Bartlesville this time about the company's fate if it lost this ownership contest. Pickens at least said he would move to Bartlesville and run the company if he gained control. Financial analyst George Sneed's chilling interpretation of Icahn's intentions made Pickens sound like a long-lost friend:

> Icahn and his backers have no interest in buying Phillips Petroleum Company to operate it. They would liquidate the company if they get control of it. They are trying to force the price up and if they can get Phillips merged or bought out at a higher price, that is what they want . . . There is an awful lot of stock in the hands of short-term speculators and they absolutely do not care what happens to Bartlesville.

While local residents disliked both corporate raiders, Icahn was generally deemed even less trustworthy and more dangerous than Pickens. Jeweler Josef Derryberry again spoke for many when he said he could not trust Icahn's remarks about his plans for Phillips: "One moment you'll keep Phillips in Bartlesville and the next moment you say you'll sell it to the highest bidder. There's only one business I know of that you can sell and keep it too," he said. Asked to compare people's reactions to Icahn and Pickens, a Phillips manager recalled:

> Pickens wasn't too well liked, but Icahn, well we really had to campaign against him . . . Pickens was a petroleum man. But Icahn, and there were several with him, had made quite a reputation and a lot of money just moving parts of companies around. They were both looked at in a different way. I think in Bartlesville they both were considered SOB's, but Boone at least was Mr. SOB.

Not everyone agrees. As one retail merchant, whose business has still not recovered, sees it, "We put Icahn and Pickens in the same classification. One was an easterner, one a southwesterner. You know, it doesn't make any difference whether you got shit on your boots or wear a bow tie. If you're a corporate raider looking for a quick profit, who cares who he is?"

On March 5, 1985, Phillips assured its independence for the foreseeable future by meeting Icahn's terms. It "sharply improved the terms" of its offer to repurchase much of the company's stock from its shareholders. To pay for it, the company took on more debt. Published estimates of Mr. Icahn's gross profit from his roughly six-week investment in Phillips stock range from $30 million to $75 million. The company also paid an additional $25 million of Icahn's expenses from their takeover fight. These included payments to "a consortium of private and institutional investors, including such active raiders as the Canadian Belzberg family, Saul Steinberg, and the Leucadia National Corporation, [which, for holding aside] $1.5 billion for about two weeks [to loan Icahn if he had needed it], received $5,625,000 in fees and never had to put up a nickel." In return, Phillips got agreements from Carl Icahn and his main Wall Street backer, Drexel Burnham Lambert, Inc., to stop trying to buy the company. Phillips' outlay, for the three months of legal and financial services it bought itself and its raiders, exceeded $200 million. Irwin Jacobs, one of Icahn's best-known allies in the just-finished battle, summed it up very well: "Phillips has bought its independence, and the town of Bartlesville can rest easy tonight."

Once again, Phillips employees and Bartlesville were relieved the company stayed independent and intact. The city had recently been in the news for mailing heart-shaped Valentine's Day cookies with the Phillips 66 shield on them to Icahn and large shareholders during the latest battle. But the mood was less joyful and more subdued than when the contest with Pickens ended. Now, Bartlesville heaved "a collective sigh of relief. 'Conservative optimism' is how the editor of the local paper describes the mood," reported the *Christian Science Monitor*. A Phillips manager recalls:

> After a while people had just sort of gotten used to it. A little jaded, probably more fatalistic. Yeah, we might be taken over. Another one just showed up with more threats, so they'll fight it out. Much of the outrage and shock was probably used up in the struggle with Pickens. Everyone was still upset, but people just got on with other things as the fights dragged on.

Six weeks after Phillips settled with Icahn, David Oakley, owner of the city's Pontiac-Buick dealership, reported that car sales were improving. "People are convinced now that there is going to be a community, although they're not sure if they're going to have a job," he said.

To remain independent and keep raiders at bay, Phillips had taken a very high stakes gamble. This was that its oil and gas, combined with the sale of assets, would keep generating enough cash to cover payments due on the billions it borrowed to buy back 50 percent of its stock.

In less than a year, the company's debt had tripled from $2.8 to $8.6 billion. Its credit rating had been lowered. Phillips's interest payments for 1985 zoomed to $846 million, more than double its earnings. Company officials, and some oil industry experts, downplayed the seriousness of the situation. Phillips planned to reduce its debt quickly by selling at least $2 billion in assets. "They've got salable stuff coming out their ears . . . [and] could get rid of $2 billion without blinking," said one industry analyst. Company Chairman William Douce acknowledged that "it's a pretty good debt load for a while, but we have a strong cash flow and that's really the name of the game." After leading his company through the two brutal takeover wars, Douce referred to himself as a "born-again debtor." "We can remain strong and vital, no question," he said.

Others were less optimistic about the firm's chances for a quick comeback. "Phillips has mortgaged its future. The price of independence is a mountain of debt," said Sanford Margoshes, senior oil analyst at Shearson/American Express. He believed that "this is a company where some of the glow has been extinguished." Many observers called Phillips's debt, now between 75 and 80 percent of its total capital, "staggering." They predicted management's energy would be absorbed more by cutting debt and expenses than by competing hard for new oil fields and customers. Phillips is "definitely a weaker competitor," said Lawrence Funkhauser, Chevron's vice president for exploration and production.

"They've got a period of four or five years to get back to where they were before Pickens attacked them." Amoco's chief economist, Ted Eck, also commented, "It's hard to see how you could be a superaggressive exploration company when you've got 75 percent debt."

The most critical wild card in Phillips's high-stakes gamble would be the price of oil. The cash flow it needed to pay off its huge debt required a minimum price of $20 per barrel. After the big stock buyback, the *Washington Post* reported:

> About the only thing analysts believe could put Phillips' rebuilding efforts out of kilter would be an unexpected drop in the price of oil. In setting up its restructuring, Phillips has assumed an average oil price for the next few years of about $27 a barrel, and a worst-case scenario of about $20 a barrel.

"If the price of oil goes down, Phillips is going to be in trouble," said oil analyst Fred Leuffer. Another analyst, who asked not to be identified, added, "If oil prices went down to $20 a barrel, Phillips faced financial peril." The experts' consensus tied Phillips's recovery to these magic numbers. If they fell below $20, that would mean lower prices for the assets Phillips needed to sell, and less cash from the sale of its own oil and gasoline. Since the company had to repay its steep loans, no matter what, the missing balance would have to come from elsewhere if oil prices did drop.

Within five months of Phillips's successful fights to stay independent, oil prices started a plunge toward $10 a barrel. The company's strategy of "borrow now, pay later" began to unravel. Its high debt and cash-poor position left it without any of the "rainy day" money companies need to tide themselves over during hard times. Phillips was more vulnerable to falling prices than any other oil company (except Unocal, which had followed

Phillips's example by also going into deep debt to fight off another bid by T. Boone Pickens). Two *Wall Street Journal* reports show how precarious the company's financial position became by the summers of 1985 and 1986:

> Bob Crawford raises his voice to be heard over a thumping oil pump he has just lubricated in the Phillips Petroleum Co. oil field here [in Shidler, Oklahoma]. "If oil prices drop farther, Phillips will have to liquidate this field and me with it," he says. For Phillips and several other major oil companies, "the crunch" came mainly from taking on massive increases in debt at a time when oil prices were slumping. The result is a double-edged sword that threatens to seriously reduce both revenue and profit in the industry.
>
> The heavy debt, low-price bug has made no big oil company sicker than Phillips. Just last year, Phillips was weathering the energy slump quite nicely. Its profit rose 12%, and its debt load was one of the lightest around. But the company's bitter takeover battles with Messrs. Pickens and Icahn earlier this year changed all that. To fend them off, Phillips borrowed $4.5 billion, raising its debt-to-equity ratio to a staggering 80%. That's easily the highest among the majors, and analysts are worried, particularly in light of falling prices.
>
> "They're over my danger line," says Kurt Wulff, a Donaldson, Lufkin & Jenrette analyst . . . Living on the edge is proving painful for the nation's eighth biggest oil company.
>
> (August 9, 1985)

> Most energy-related companies have been forced to cut costs sharply because of the oil price plunge, but Unocal and Phillips are in especially difficult positions . . . "they're hanging on with bloody fingers at this point," says [analyst] Alan Edgar . . .
>
> For its part, Phillips has taken drastic steps in light of lower oil prices. Its work force has been

> cut by 3,400 employees, to 21,900, since the first of the year.
>
> (July 28,1986)

In Bartlesville, Phillips acknowledged that by summer 1985, it was using up oil reserves faster than it was replacing them. "If we continued that way, it would make us self-liquidating," said Bill Thompson, vice president for planning and development. "It's like having a house that takes four gallons of paint and you've got only three—the house will look like hell." A common feeling managers expressed was that budget reductions were cutting into the bone of their operations. For example:

> Staffing and operations have been cut back to a point where I can no longer function smoothly. This happened just as markets became chaotic because of falling oil prices. So now we are missing business we should be getting because we just can't handle it. And it's not because people are lazy or stupid, people are working very hard at nights and on weekends. I work feverishly all day and then bring a briefcase full of work home and work until 10:30 or so every night, and still can't keep up. If things stay like this, Phillips has a serious problem, because we can't continue as we are.

Referring back to the takeover battles, the same manager says, "We've done the equivalent of somebody who was threatened by a mugger, sitting there slashing your wrist so you scare them off with all the blood. We don't have the strength to go out and lift weights anymore. We've had to pull back our operations and try to conserve cash as much as possible."

Mr. Pickens was not convinced the company's operations had been streamlined far enough. His recommendations in both summer 1985 and 1986 reportedly suggested that Phillips should continue "slimming the . . . payroll" and "cut their costs and trim exploration budgets before cutting dividends further."

Phillips Petroleum has retained its independence, but the price of victory was very high for the company, its employees, and the people of Bartlesville. Many jobs were lost, and for those remaining the company is a much leaner "home away from home." The takeover battles also left scars on the community at large. One of the city's leading retailers believes the experience "destroyed a part of" its spirit. John Norell, president of a Phillips research subsidiary, wrote in a letter to the U.S. House Energy and Commerce Committee, "There is something fundamentally wrong in America that a $16 billion company who is financially strong and interested in long-range developments for itself, the country, and humanity on one day can then on the next day, after a run on it by Mr. T. Boone Pickens, be reduced to a debt-ridden, short term, and cost-cutting entity."

Oil industry analyst Sanford Margoshes spoke for many when he said, "As a member of the planet I would say one should not be pleased with a proliferation of this type of development."

Part One. How Wall Street Helped Kill Loyalty and Commitment

1. Dismantling the Fortune 500: The New War on Managers

America's mightiest firms are firing thousands of our most talented managers. At the same time, the number of management positions at large U.S. corporations is falling. Like Phillips Petroleum, other big companies have been crippled, stripped down against the best judgment of their own top executives during a decade of retrenchment. Between 1980 and 1990, it is estimated that more than one million managers will have lost their jobs. With more and more companies being forced to accelerate cost cutting and avoid taking entrepreneurial risks, the number of attractive management positions on the career ladder has nosedived.

These actions are destroying the lives of loyal long-term managers, the people who know a company's business best and are most committed to its continued success. The corporation's commitment to its own people has fallen at every level to the lowest point in fifty years. This slide has happened so quickly that it is still catching managers off guard.

Both ambitious young managers and their superiors see talented co-workers being held back or dismissed. The lesson they are learning is to avoid making a commitment to a company or caring how well the company does in the future. Today's managers must be tough; they are being pushed by these changes to pursue a more self-protective, "me-first" definition of their careers.

Big companies began to cut back on offering their most promising managers attractive promotions during the 1980s when a powerful new trio of corporate strategies—Downsize, Dismantle, and Debt—became popular. Corporations stopped expanding into new lines of business once they were infected by the debilitating presumptions of these new strategies. Top managers were quickly transformed into accountants and finance men. When this happens, already approved operations must be shelved if they promise only long-run payoffs, require new investment, or yield margins requiring any patience. Short-run action replaces long-term vision.

Every big company has good reason to fear being captured by this type of thinking. According to the rules of Downsize, Dismantle, and Debt, many giant firms among the Fortune 500 would be worth more dead than alive. In accounting language, a company becomes "undervalued" whenever the total value of its shares drops below the total value of its assets. Speculators can then purchase the firm's stock, fire employees, and immediately sell off its plants, equipment, and real estate for more than they paid to buy the company. Since stock prices rise and fall unpredictably, corporations are constantly vulnerable to this shock treatment. A rapid decline easily puts a company on the auction block with little advance warning. At these times, large institutional investors and their money managers cannot resist the temptation to force painful selloffs and "restructurings" on companies with good cash flows, high book value, low share price, and liquid assets. Every large company is at risk.

Major firms not being acquired or weakened by steep drops in their share price are already dismantling themselves, dismissing workers and using the money they save in employee salaries to raise their stock price by buying their own shares. Dozens of speculators from the financial world are watching from their computer terminals, waiting to pounce on companies that resist restructuring themselves. Large clienteles of investors and other big corporations on the prowl for new acquisitions pay lucrative fees to investment bankers for developing exactly this type of information.

Once a company's number comes up, it takes only a short time before its assets are sold off. Many proud, blue-chip names that have long stood for money and power have already been stripped down to their bare essentials—names such as Gulf, Revlon, Goodyear, CBS and Gillette. Think of how companies like

these long provided world-renowned models of successful corporations with strong product lines, power, prestige, and smart business sense. Just to be able to tell people they worked for one of these companies allowed employees to share and take pride in their glamour and high reputations. Few managers suspected they would fall victim to a takeover or restructuring executed by a financial wizard they had never heard of before. Too many managers are still learning the hard way that when companies change hands, downsize, or restructure, anyone in the company can land out on the street.

Consider Tom Grady's collision with these new corporate realities. Grady was a top-performing salesman for the industrial products division of a large, recently acquired company:

> On Valentine's Day, 1985, Tom heard there would be some announcements about transfers and relocations. He didn't think any of his friends would be moved but was curious to see whose jobs would be affected. Tom's own division was safe. Its high profitability pleased the company's new owners, who said it would continue running its own shop. At 1:30, a cleancut new Group VP called a meeting of Tom's group. This VP smiled and said their new CEO was so pleased with last quarter's results that he decided to immediately put his consultant's exciting new master plan into effect. Operations were going to be combined throughout the entire corporate family. Grady's unit would soon join two other divisions to form an important new strategic business unit.
>
> Tom definitely didn't like what he was hearing. He tuned back in for "After all, since we all work for the same company now it's clear that the sooner we merge these old divisions the better off we'll be." Then came the punch lines. Design and development staff for his division would be transferred from San Francisco to Cleveland, where the other divisions were located. Unfortunately, some

> production managers in California would have to be laid off, due to excess capacity in the Midwest. All marketing, sales, and distribution would be handled by the other divisions as well.
>
> In plain English, Tom Grady was fired. Just like that. No warning. Nothing personal, of course. He had won the company's award for Best Salesman last year, but would have to remember it was a different company back then. After the takeover, he had believed the assurances about the division being left alone. Grady had not updated his résumé, and had not answered headhunters' invitations to consider switching companies. He liked his job, and was good at it, and had felt no desire to leave.
>
> Tom Grady was given four months' severance pay and two weeks to clear out. He could not imagine how new people with no firsthand knowledge of the division's technically complex products would hold on to his customer base. He had built it up very carefully for the company but was fired without even being asked to leave information about key West Coast accounts, or for any suggestions about servicing them from Ohio. "Well, thanks a lot and to hell with you, too," Grady thought. But he also knew "that's eight years of my life they just threw away, without even a personal phone call to say sorry, or even thanks. Damn!"

Tom Grady was hit very hard by this brutal firing. Totally unprepared, he believed what he was told, and had put off considering his options and alternatives. But not having thought much about them certainly didn't make Grady any safer when "it" happened to him. Most managers are like Tom Grady in his avoidance of thinking uncomfortable thoughts about "what if" situations. Thousands of managers and workers who have been fired outright, laid off, or pushed into early retirement in this wave of restructurings simply didn't believe it would happen to them either.

This disenfranchisement of the managerial class, and the dashing of its expectations, threaten the long-run health and productivity of corporate America. They challenge the essential basis for any long-term relationship between a company and its employees—trust in each others's promises and integrity.

We are living in the midst of a wrenching shift, leading to a situation in which managers must think of themselves as free agents. The concept of Free Agent Managers, already known from professional sports, has nasty implications for company loyalty and corporate cultures. When managers can no longer trust their employers, they spend more time planning their own futures and less time concerned about their company's. Productivity declines and performance suffers. Wholesale dismissals of high performers like Tom Grady have sent managers the clear message that long-standing rules tying their promotions and careers to one employer have been changed without warning. One can no longer safely expect companies to reciprocate loyalty and trust them to care about career plans, hopes, and dreams for the future. In response to this much meaner corporate climate, managers need to pack their own parachutes.

The Battle to Redefine the Corporation

Embattled corporate executives have repressed their best instincts and allowed these disasters to strike many of their most valuable managers because they think this may "save" their companies from being forced to take even more drastic measures. There's a deadly serious war on. At issue is who gets to define the very purpose of the corporation.

Lined up on one side are the forces of tradition: corporate managements, employees, and the many communities in which they live and work. Each of these groups has a stake in the stability, continued growth, and long-term success of the giant companies they have known for years. Their view of the company's mission requires it to be profitable, but also expects it to retain a significant portion of earnings and capital for cash reserves, investments in long-range projects, new business ventures, and contributions to community institutions. They can hardly imagine them no longer around to continue developing and producing goods, services, jobs, and wealth for present and future generations. Indeed, the jobs of more than one out of three persons employed today in the United States depend directly on the continued health and existence of fewer than 1,000 of these corporate giants.

Attacking this traditional view is a powerful convergence of Wall Street bankers, high-ranking government bureaucrats, and influential consultants forging a strike force demanding drastic cutbacks in the size of large corporations. Their hostile attack challenges the value, competence, and credibility of companies and their managers. Executives are attacked for creating inefficient, unimaginative, bloated "corpocracies," and characterized as failures. This is certainly an abrupt change after years of their having been praised for providing new products and jobs for the work force.

While verbal wars over corporate value and performance rage on, this redefinition places Fortune 500 managers, once in secure positions with promising career paths, at considerable risk. In fewer than five years, the threat of unexpected downsizings, restructurings, mergers, divestments, and stock buybacks has reduced career planning to a random crapshoot.

Among the major forces backing this negative redefinition of the corporation, an important source of political support has been Washington's seven-year-long green light for giant mergers, which inevitably require restructuring some part of the new entity. Deregulation, combined with the relaxation of antitrust prohibitions by the Reagan administration, have encouraged some of the largest megamergers in over sixty years. Oil giants, such as Gulf and Getty, have been acquired by other oil companies; Eastern and other airlines have been swallowed by former competitors; banking is undergoing nationwide consolidations; and big corporations are being captured by even bigger companies, such as RCA's acquisition by GE.

A second political force emerged in 1986 as a chorus of government officials sought to sidetrack calls for a change in U.S. trade policy. Rather than address the issues of other nations blocking American exports and dumping products here, high-ranking bureaucrats in the U.S. Departments of Commerce, Labor, and the Treasury mounted harsh attacks on "risk-averse," "short-sighted" American managements. This rush to oversimplify complex trade problems and intimidate companies and managers fighting subsidized foreign competition led to further cutbacks and firings.

Washington's harsh political rhetoric is driven home by the more consistent economic and philosophical position advanced by Wall Street since 1980. This redefinition pressures corporations to "restructure or liquidate, but get all profits to shareholders now!" It criticizes managements for caring as much about their companies' products and employees as about higher earnings and stock prices. Joined by a host of consultants and other critics, Wall Street portrays large corporations as wasteful, witless dinosaurs in need of downsizings and management shakeups. These draconian remedies, not just coincidentally, mean instant jumps in share price and ensure enormous fees and stock trading profits for Wall Street.

The economic redefinition asserts the sole obligation of top managements, at large firms with publicly traded stock, is to continually increase the company's share price. They must achieve this by whatever means necessary, whether that involves taking on huge debt to buy back enough shares to raise the value of those still remaining, or firing employees to cut payrolls, or selling off divisions and lines of business to generate more cash.

This short-term perspective is wildly popular with Wall Street brokerage houses, money center banks, big mutual and pension funds, and professional investors and speculators. Since every big name in high finance has joined the corporate restructuring bandwagon, from Merrill Lynch, Citibank, First Boston Corporation, and Prudential Insurance, to Sears, General Electric, T. Boone Pickens, and American Express, there is no question that large companies are aware of the close attention being accorded their current share price. As John Nevin, chairman of the Firestone Tire and Rubber Company, put it, "Managers are much more aware now than 10 years ago they've got to generate wealth for their shareholders, or they will be in jeopardy of losing control of the corporations they run."

This drastically narrowed perspective on what makes up a company, reducing its entire meaning to its current share price, has had a remarkable impact on the behavior of many top corporate executives. Some have reacted by abandoning the long-run and choosing one of the "Downsize, Dismantle, and Debt" strategies recommended by this myopic new definition. A few companies, such as Arco Petroleum, embraced all three at once and became shells of their former selves. Other firms, such as the large holding company City Investing, simply self-liquidated by selling off their own assets rather than letting others come along to do it for them. In all of these cases, the value of the dismembered companies' shares jumped dramatically for a short time. "In essence," as reporter Daniel Cuff and oil analyst Sanford Margoshes noted about Phillips Petroleum's stock buyback, these companies liquidated "a part of [themselves] to bring future benefits to shareholders now. 'In this sense, the long-term shareholder has been injured because the long-term stream of benefits has been diminished.'"

Restructuring the Corporation into a "Cash Cow"

Long before managers ever heard of corporate raiders, restructurings were normal events in American business. A "restructuring" occurred whenever a company undertook new financial arrangements that significantly impacted its operations and employees. A new company with unusually strong sales and profits, such as Lotus [software] Development Corporation, restructures by raising huge sums for expansion through a large public stock offering. A less fortunate firm, drowning in red ink, restructures by severely contracting, as in the case of LTV, one of the largest corporations ever to declare bankruptcy in the United States.

Restructurings provide necessary mechanisms for keeping the firm's operational performance in line with its financial condition. The market has long rewarded strong performance with high credit ratings and greater access to loans on attractive terms, thus giving managements greater flexibility in running the corporation. Poor performance is routinely punished by lenders reluctant to offer unsecured credit lines and low interest loans to high-risk borrowers. Loss of lenders' confidence usually signals a forthcoming round of layoffs, executive resignations or firings, and general belt-tightening.

The new financial perspective advanced by Wall Street bankers and securities analysts conceives of the corporation as a "cash cow." Its sole purpose is to produce, right now and by whatever means necessary, the highest share price for its current owners. Wall Street's success in generating support for tearing down large companies to raise share prices constitutes a fundamental shift in how we define the very purpose of a corporation. This shift challenges the view that giant companies are living resources for the long run, requiring and entitled to at least some recognition and protection to enable them to continue making contributions to their markets, employees, and communities. In this traditional view, big companies can still go bankrupt or be taken over, but the process is expected to take longer than a "Wall Street weekend." Chrysler Corporation is a good example of a company that would not have been allowed to survive under the short-run dictum: "Restructure or liquidate, but get all the profits to shareholders now!"

Whatever new policy it takes to enforce the "cash cow" redefinition on big companies and their managers is called a restructuring. In the new financial perspective, this has become an umbrella term to describe a wide variety of painful actions taken by corporations to pacify and enrich short-term investors. If selling off a corporation's assets today will raise more cash than keeping it in business, then that is its managers' first obligation. If the financial dairy will pay less than the stockyard, in other words, the corporate cow should be milked dry and then quickly auctioned off. After all, the future is here and the short term is now.

Management experts attack this thinking as dangerously shortsighted, forcing corporations to concentrate resources and talent on short-term financial maneuvers, rather than on economically sound and socially responsible longer-term issues. Says Harvard Business School authority Jay Lorsch:

> At a time when top managers should focus on improving their long term competitive position, many have to devote immense amounts of time [to precisely these short-term financial maneuvers] . . . My . . . research has shown that top managers of successful companies concern themselves much more with the long-term health of their companies. In almost every case, the executives have spent their entire careers with the companies they lead and they have a strong commitment to long-term corporate well-being . . . Their primary motives are for the long-term benefit of all the company's constituents. . . .

Professor Warren Law, also at Harvard, notes pointedly, "The corporation is not a piece of paper and should not be bought and sold in that way . . . [The] belief that human and physical capital is no more real than pieces of paper in a stock portfolio . . . [is] dangerous."

Another of America's foremost management scholars, Peter Drucker, is a sharp critic of the "cash cow" perspective. He predicts that this view of the corporation will outlast the recent wave of "hostile takeovers." Drucker is especially concerned about its negative effects on current and future generations of managers:

> Corporate managements are being pushed into subordinating everything (even such long-range considerations as a company's market standing, its technology, indeed its basic wealth-producing capacity) to immediate earnings and next week's stock price.
>
> [This] contributes to the . . . slighting of tomorrow in research, product development, and in quality and service—all to squeeze out a few more dollars in next quarter's "bottom line." But also, employees from senior managers down to the rank and file in the office or factory floor, are increasingly being demoralized—a thoughtful union leader of my acquaintance calls it "traumatized"—by [this] fear . . . Anyone working with management people knows that fear [of these short-term demands] paralyzes our executives. Worse, it forces them into making decisions they know to be stupid and to damage the enterprise in their charge. . . .
>
> Abatement of the boom in hostile takeovers can, paradoxically, only aggravate the . . . problem . . . [by putting] even greater pressure for quick results on [pension fund managers who], in turn will [demand more] short-term results [from the companies whose shares they own]—thus pushing business even further towards managing for short term.

The "Cash Cow" Corporation and the Disposable Manager

The "cash cow" definition of the firm devalues and distrusts managers. Its proponents regard managers' concerns for the company's continued success as "inefficient" and sentimental—even "irresponsible." Managers stand in the way of instantly increasing the company's value and share price because they oppose such instant cash-raisers as selling off key divisions and slashing budgets by 30 percent. The "cash cow" definition revels in managers' job insecurity ("Keeps 'em on their toes!") and ties productivity rises to work force reductions and pay cuts.

The clash between these competing definitions of the corporation is illustrated by the recommendations of management experts William Ouchi, in his book *Theory Z,* and Tom Peters and Robert Waterman, in their book *In Search of Excellence.* Opposed to the destructiveness of the "cash cow" perspective, these authors argued for higher trust levels between managers and their corporations as the basis for increasing creativity, commitment, and productivity. They noted that companies that perform best over time and produce fiercely loyal employees share a large number of important attributes. These include supporting new ideas and risk-taking, providing challenging environments where jobs are not always on the line, and developing distinctive company cultures with in-house career ladders.

The "cash cow" redefinition, with its dogged emphasis on short-term balance sheets and share price, has no place for imagining the corporation as a generous workplace where ideas such as trust and the long-term remain honored and credible. Instead, today's managers are jolted by new "cash cow" euphemisms for firing, such as "surplusing," "downsizing," "demassing," "flattening the hierarchy," "getting lean and mean," and "restructuring." Accompanying a recent *Business Week* feature on the "End of Corporate Loyalty," a concerned editorial noted:

> Companies can find many ways to get rid of people, and these days corporations are using them all . . . Corporate America is caught up in a frantic drive to reduce its work force, mostly to save money, but also to slim down into what top management hopes will be a more *responsive* structure [my italics].

The extraordinary act of firing so many people is "responsive" largely to demands from the world of high finance to immediately raise share price by cutting costs now. Wall Street's advice to managers searching for excellence, put simply, has been to tell them to become excellent at searching for new jobs.

Managers have every right to be nervous and act to protect themselves in a climate where consultants advise corporations to *discourage* managers from feeling that the company is their "home away from home." Experts recognize that the relationship between corporations and their managers is growing fragile, that fewer companies can be wholly trusted by their employees. The impact of destroying this long-standing psychological contract is captured by management consultant Wilton Murphy: "Companies have made a unilateral change in the rules of the game. More large organizations in effect are telling their people, 'You have skills we currently need; we have a job available. As long as that's there, we have a relationship—but don't count on anything beyond that.'"

Estimates vary on how many people and families have already been touched by this drastic change in the working rules in today's corporations, but all agree the numbers are too large to ignore. From the available evidence, a conservative conclusion is in just the four years between 1983 and 1987, well over two million people saw their jobs disappear or deteriorate as a result of takeovers, forced mergers, and other restructurings. During this same time, nearly 10,000 companies traded hands, impacting the millions of workers and managers on their payrolls. *Fortune* estimates that merging two companies directly affects one-quarter to one-half of all employees in both organizations. If statistics were collected on the human consequences of treating companies as no more than cash cows, adds *Fortune* editorial board member Myron Magnet, they would "show how many employees get relocated, lose jobs, status, benefits, or opportunities, are drained of commitment or self-esteem, or develop health or family problems." In an economy as interdependent and deregulated as ours, these problems are not confined to any single industry or sector. The 200 largest megamergers since 1983 wrought changes affecting the work lives of over ten million people. The ripple effect extends those changes to millions of more jobs, and nearby businesses and service organizations, ranging from material suppliers, retail establishments, and messenger services, to hospitals and United Way.

The financial wizards of Wall Street, however, dismiss the problems created by restructurings as just another cost of doing business. "Besides," some like to add, "the managements probably deserved it." Among managers' harshest critics in the army of high finance, the most hostile are corporate raiders, many of whom have little experience managing anything more complex than their own stock portfolios. Raiders fault managers for acting against the best interest of shareholders and misusing corporate assets. They claim managers have only themselves to blame when their firms become takeover targets. "These managements need shaking up—they're horrendous," says Carl Icahn, who also compares them to gardeners hired to work on the shareholders' estates. "That's all these guys are, you know—the gardeners," Icahn told a reporter from TWA's *Ambassador* magazine less than a year before he and his investor group "hijacked" the entire company in a surprise takeover.

Sir James Goldsmith, the British investor who joined with Merrill Lynch in 1986 to launch an attack on the Goodyear Tire & Rubber Company, states that "No excellent company is subject to a takeover. . . . The only companies running that risk are those where the market, in its wisdom, thinks management is not making its assets work best," he insists. The impact of this powerful financial perspective, as T. Boone Pickens notes, is that "managements are going to be a hell of a lot more interested in the price of stock in the marketplace." He sees this as a useful corrective to their chief executives' having "no more feeling for the average shareholder than they do for baboons in Africa."

Managers and their families are not the only people to suffer in the employee firings that follow "cash cow" power grabs and

A Glossary of Merger and Takeover Terminology

Ambush	Swift and premeditated takeover attempt.
Barricades	Impediments to a takeover (usually lawsuits) raised by the target company ("throwing up the barricades").
Bear hug	Hostile tender offer, usually with considerable muscle behind it.
Big-game hunting	Plotting and executing takeovers of large companies.
Big-hat boys	Texas moneymen interested in big-game hunting.
Black book	A point-by-point antitakeover plan that every potential target is presumed to have ready at all times.
Black knights	Unfriendly acquirers drawn to a target by news that the company is already being propositioned by others.
Chess	Description of takeover activity as a game, used by investment bankers.
Chinese wall	Internal procedures to prevent communication of privileged information between bank lending officers and trust department staff. Gaps in the Chinese wall are objects of fear and resentment by takeover targets.
Confetti	Stock traded by acquirer for that of acquiree, particularly if thought of as having little value.
Cyanide pill	Antitakeover finance strategy in which the potential target arranges for long-term debt to fall due immediately and in full if it is acquired.
Double Pac-Man strategy	Target firm makes tender offer for the stock of its would-be acquirer; employed by Martin Marietta against Bendix Corporation.
Faye	Code name used by Sol Steinberg's Leasco Corporation in Chemical Bank takeover dis-

	cussions, taken from actress Faye Dunaway's role as bank robber in *Bonnie and Clyde*.
Fight letter	Strong declaration of target company's opposition to a raider's offer; a gloves-off fight is likely to follow.
Golden parachutes	Provision in the employment contracts of top executives that assures them a lucrative financial landing if the firm is acquired in a takeover.
Gray knight	A rescuer no more desirable than the initial raider and less attractive than a white knight.
Greenmail	A firm's purchase of its own stock, at a premium, from an investor who it fears will otherwise seek to acquire it or else initiate a proxy fight to oust its present management.
Hired guns	Merger and acquisition specialists, other investment bankers, and lawyers employed by either side in any takeover.
Jaws	The powerful shark of movie fame, transformed into a predatory takeover artist.
Junk bonds	High-risk, high-yield debt certificates traded publicly, so called because they are rated below investment grade, either by Moody's or by Standard & Poor's; a specialty of Drexel Burnham, junk bonds are often used to help finance hostile takeovers.
Monopoly	Game image used by hired guns engaged in takeover activity.
Mushroom treatment	Postmerger problems from an acquired executive's standpoint: "first they buried us in manure, then they left us in the dark awhile, then they let us stew, and finally they canned us" (Barmash, 1971).
Pigeons	Highly vulnerable targets.
Pirates	Hostile acquirers.
Raiders	Hostile acquirers.
Saturday night special	A fast and predatory merger; originated with Colt's swift takeover of Garlock.

Scorched earth	A policy whereby the target company would rather self-destruct than be acquired (e.g., all personnel threaten to quit). The scorched earth strategy also involves a hearty mud-slinging campaign directed at the raiding company.
Seed partner	Big investor committed to the firm as is, whose large ownership protects a potential target company from acquisition.
Sex without marriage	Extended negotiations for a friendly merger that never takes place.
Shark repellent	Protective strategies for preventing or combating a hostile tender offer.
Sleeping beauties	Vulnerable targets.
Summer soldier	Executive of target company offering only token resistance against a takeover.
Takeover	The purchase of majority ownership in a corporation; usually resisted by the target company but accomplished nonetheless by paying a premium above the current market price for the firm's shares.
Target	Corporation selected for takeover by a would-be acquirer.
Tender offer	Proposal to purchase a firm's stock from its shareholders for an amount higher than its current market price.
Tombstones	Advertisements in the financial press containing announcements of interest to investors and the business community (e.g., tender offers, stock underwritings, mergers, and divestments).
Unfriendly offer	Proposal to transfer a firm's ownership to parties viewed as hostile or unworthy by its current board and executives; usually resisted and seldom endorsed by the target company.

White knight	Acceptable acquirer sought by a potential target to forestall an unfriendly takeover; the preferred suitor.
Wounded list	Executives of an acquired firm who develop health or career problems from the deal.

corporate restructurings. The surrounding communities and their economies also are threatened and stand to lose when the "cash cow" redefinition is foisted upon large companies in local areas. "'Icahn has raped this community . . . ,' [exclaims] Elsie C. Slayton, a resident of Danville, Virginia, whose largest employer, Dan River, Inc., was the subject of a 1983 Icahn takeover attempt." Like Phillips Petroleum, Dan River went into enormous debt to buy back its stock at inflated prices and restructure itself. It has "since slashed 2,000 local jobs. Plummeting retail sales have decimated the downtown area, says Mayor C. Miller Vernon."

In Pittsburgh, the nation's third largest city for corporate headquarters, there was shock and dismay in 1986 when Icahn targeted U.S. Steel, recently renamed USX Corporation. This industrial giant had reported revenues of $19 billion in the last year and employed nearly 10,000 people in the Pittsburgh area. Many wondered how someone who probably had never set foot in a steel mill could operate the nation's fifteenth largest corporation more skillfully than its managers. This did not trouble like-minded moneymen on Wall Street, where Icahn succeeded in lining up nearly $7 billion to pursue USX. He added still more to his war chest by "using the cash and borrowing power of Trans World Airlines and ACF Industries, Inc.," two companies he had conquered earlier.

Pittsburgh's Mayor Caliguiri urged the city's residents to boycott TWA flights. The *Wall Street Journal* reported, "Pittsburgh Shudders at Icahn Proposal to Acquire USX," explaining that

> USX dominates the city, from its 64-story corporate headquarters, the tallest building here, to its ownership stake in the Pittsburgh Pirates baseball team and support of local institutions such as the Pittsburgh Symphony Society and University of Pittsburgh. "USX has been the single strongest corporate structure here for decades and [a takeover] would be the single worst thing that could happen to our corporate landscape," says Justin T. Horan, president of the Greater Pittsburgh Chamber of Commerce.

Even though Wall Street "enforcers" like Icahn may only accelerate restructurings already under way, the surrounding communities invariably suffer from the unplanned destruction these rapid upheavals leave behind them.

The Impact of Restructuring on Managers: The Human Cost

Back in 1984, one of the most spectacular deals of the year was the merger of two of America's largest food companies, Beatrice and Esmark. The deal was widely celebrated as friendly, with a carefully designed script arranged to assure a happy ending for all. Each company board blessed the proposed ownership change, and Esmark's shareholders reaped handsome premiums from the sale of the company. Many managers believed all the promises they had received and were confident that the merger couldn't possibly end like the vicious battle they had just seen decimate Gulf Oil.

Then the carnage began. As retold by one Esmark executive, "We got memo after memo from [Beatrice Chairman] that we weren't to worry; we would all have jobs since this was a true merger and not an acquisition. And then they wiped out whole [Esmark] departments." Today, the events that occurred at Beatrice and Esmark are more the rule than the exception. Nearly 60 percent of corporate marriages end in disaster. Too often, the market share and financial performance of the acquired company drop after the merger, and the clash of different corporate cultures frequently leads to unexpected mutual hostility and incomprehension.

The last question usually asked in a merger is "How will the combined organizations be managed?" This is because the premerger discussions focus almost exclusively on how the deal will be financed. Even when there is plenty of time to plan out the postmerger organization, the attention of bankers and Wall Street professionals stays riveted on the dowries of tax-loss carryforwards and other financial assets offered by present or potential corporate damsels in distress. "Softer" matters, such as people with jobs on the line, receive far less careful analysis. Employees are treated as details expected to fall in place later, settle themselves, or just go away.

Restructurings are the biggest disruption to hit companies and their managers since the Great Depression. Experts expect their explosive pace to continue dramatically for the foreseeable future. "We're not even a tenth of the way into the kind of restructuring we're going to see," says James Farley, senior chairman of Booz Allen & Hamilton, one of the world's premier consulting firms.

Every restructuring costs jobs and sends people packing. "Restructuring" is the code word most often used by companies to mask the hurt and destruction being forced on their managers. The major shift in corporate priorities, away from the operations-based long-range perspective of managements, to the short-term profit-taking demands of the financial community, translates into personal disaster for those caught by surprise in companies that restructure.

Once a restructuring is announced, it is guaranteed to traumatize almost everyone throughout the corporation. Everything grinds to a halt. Executives abandon plans for the company's future and worry about setting up financial deals to raise the company's current share price. Managers stop minding the store. Everyone knows that from here on out there will be less growth, more debt, and fewer decent top jobs. This is the time to come to terms with the fact that even if the name stays the same, it will no longer be the same company to work for.

To any manager caught in the crossfire brought on by "Downsize, Dismantle, and Debt," it will not matter which financial buzzword claims responsibility for terrorizing his or her company. The effect on a company's work force will be the same, whether the restructuring is caused by a takeover, buyback, divestment, leveraged buyout, or merger. All of these events translate into financial manipulation, a deadly game managers experience on a personal level.

For the thousands of managers and workers fired outright, laid off, or pushed into early retirement, restructurings are simply a personal tragedy. Like Tom Grady, few of the men and women cut loose ever believed it would happen to them. They couldn't imagine that AT&T would reach out and fire them, or that other "model employers," such as Kodak, DuPont, Exxon, Ford, Heinz, Warner Lambert, and CBS would invite their employees to retire early, or simply tell them, "Sorry, but you no longer have a job here."

Rudolph Dew, vice president of Hay Career Consultants, has helped many traumatized managers deal with their shock and grief, restore their confidence, and develop a less naive attitude for the next job. Sitting in his Los Angeles office, he told me, "Even when people know it's coming, they don't plan. The most common famous last words are 'We'll have enough notice.'" Dew describes some of the most common adverse reactions seen by outplacement counselors:

- *Disbelief: People Can't Believe They've Been Fired.* "They forget what they were told and remember only about 20 percent of the whole conversation. Their dismissals are almost never performance-based."
- *Panic.* "Psychologists don't know how sick it feels. You have to have experienced it. Your

power base is gone, your identity shattered, your routine destroyed. You have no office to go to. You certainly can't go to the club. You don't even have a business card anymore."

- *Stress.* "Absolutely no question about it. We caution everyone we see to get a medical checkup and to exercise. These people start catching colds. They need to be built back up and helped to fight off depression. The most important point is to always focus on the future."
- *Depression: Older Managers Have Their Whole Lives Turned Upside Down.* "After years of success—promotions, security, moves up the ladder—they're being told something they never heard before: 'You're a failure.'"
- *Vulnerability: Younger Managers Are Caught Unprepared.* "These folks, from five to eight years at their jobs, have not thought about how to write out an application. Or else they've forgotten how. They'll need to know how to respond to questions like 'What did you like best about your last job?'"
- *Fear: Scary Money Problems May Arise.* "People are unprepared not only emotionally but also financially. Since you expect your salary and raise for next year, you spend it. Losing it can hit very hard."

When managers learn that their companies are rumored to be attractive merger or takeover candidates, they often watch and wait to see how things turn out before taking some action to protect themselves. Often, the easiest, and what mistakenly may seem like the most loyal, reaction is to sit back and root for the home team against the invading marauders. That's wrong.

While hoping your employer scores all touchdowns, it is important to start checking around to learn what alternative positions may be available for you elsewhere. This does not obligate you to take any of them, of course, or to leave your firm. It means you act like a free agent. You establish a safety net, so that if you want or need to bail out of your current position in three months, the task of finding another job does not catch you completely unprepared.

If you learn that a corporate raider is buying shares of your employer's stock, or that a merger and downsizing may be on the way, reread Mr. Dew's devastating description of how you might be feeling in three months. Sitting around not taking action makes you a volunteer to join the brigade of corporate casualties he describes so well. Rather than invite the worst to happen by simply waiting, take care of yourself by having your parachute packed for the very real possibility that you may need it.

Even if the company fends off the raider or chooses its own merger partner, you should consider your options and think about leaving. While many companies have launched "successful" counterattacks and kicked the fox out of their chicken coop, smart Free Agent Managers know that is not yet the time to break out the champagne and start celebrating. They know that the high price targeted companies must pay to remain independent is hardly less painful than the drastic restructurings threatened by the raider in the first place.

The Corporate Cost of Restructuring

Wall Street's attempt to create corporate cash cows has placed an extraordinary burden on American business. More and more companies have been forced to restructure by piling on extra long-term debt. This makes corporate managers uncomfortable; they usually oppose "leveraging" their company beyond 40 percent of its liquidation value. And for good reason. The 40 percent limit provides a "rainy day" cushion for hard times, permitting additional borrowing on the substantial value of the remaining assets. It also reduces the immediate impact of poor results on existing credit arrangements, enabling the firm to overcome short-term setbacks, wait out economic downturns, and retain valued employees rather than lose them through firings.

Heavy borrowing concerns managers because, as Phillips Petroleum found after mortgaging 70 percent of itself, the only way out of hard times then becomes asset fire sales and massive employee cutbacks. Managers worry about big debt loads because their concerns for the company are usually for its long haul. Their interest collides with that of short-term investors, who have no stake in the firm's future, are not employed by it, and will not even own shares in it when the loans come due. But the managers expect to be there, and they know that when highly leveraged companies run out of collateral and cannot keep up their cash flows, banks can foreclose and require that their jobs and divisions be liquidated.

Management's concerns are rejected by investors who prefer the now-dominant "cash cow" definition of the corporation. "The company that isn't highly leveraged is not doing its job in maximizing the return to shareholders," says Irwin L. Kellner, an economist at Manufacturers Hanover Trust Company. If employees must be terminated to do this, and valued assets sold off, that's somebody else's problem.

This redefinition of "worthy" companies turns traditional thinking on its head about what a restructuring means. In the past, the "good" company retained earnings, set aside cash reserves, and kept debt to a minimum, but today, the "cash cow" company has low cash reserves, few retained earnings, and an unbearable debt load. It insists the financially secure and cash-rich firm suffer the same kind of negative restructuring formerly reserved for poor performers. It is this experience that destroys the confidence and financial edge that managers and companies expect to achieve with high performance, which should provide more slack or breathing room.

Everyone expects corporate shakeups to occur when firms respond to setbacks such as steep drops in sales or profits. While employees are disappointed when this happens, all involved can take some comfort from having tried hard for a company that, like International Harvester or Wickes Furniture, they knew was already in trouble. What managers find painful and insulting today is that they are constantly vulnerable to a restructuring, regardless of how fine a job they have done, how impressive their company's finances, or how high its reputation for good management and quality products.

Instead of rewarding good companies with infusions of new equity capital for continued growth and expansion, the "cash cow" redefinition saddles them with heavy debt loads and downgraded bond ratings. This forces management's attention away from future business development and onto cutbacks simply to service the new debt. It forces managers of well-run firms to reverse course and, as Champion International Chairman Andrew Sigler aptly puts it, "do all the things we used to consider bad management."

The "cash cow" redefinition attacks the traditionally "good" company's prudent stewardship as the callous denial of short-term investors' ownership rights. It demands that managers, instead of talking so much about the company's future, distribute its surpluses back to the shareholders right now, by borrowing more on its assets, squeezing out more cash, and pushing up short-term earnings.

Art Buchwald has a wonderful description of this fashionable new method for tearing down good companies (see box).

Managers who may have excellent reasons for opposing a "cash cow" restructuring are often discredited as greedy and self-serving. Managers, we're told, oppose seeing firms dismembered only so they can remain "entrenched" and in charge. "I'm amused by people who say that if an arbitrageur bought a stock an hour ago, he should not have the right to decide what happens to 40,000 employees," says T. Boone Pickens. Fred Hartley is one

ART BUCHWALD

Tale of Survival in the Takeover Jungle

There was a time when any American company worth its salt would be happy to proclaim it made high profits and held large cash reserves in the bank. No more. Our captains of industry are now scared to death when they have to announce they're operating in the black.

Boomer Cogswell, chairman of Dapperdan Foods, who just announced his company had lost $230 million, is an example of the new type of executive whiz kid.

I assumed Cogswell would be depressed when the news of his losses was reported. But I was wrong. He was elated. "If we luck out and have a lousy third quarter we could drop a billion dollars this year."

"And that pleases you?"

"Why wouldn't it? Last year we showed a net profit of $750 million and had $800 million in cash stashed away in the bank. Every gunslinger in America wanted to take over the company. Our glowing balance sheet threatened our very existence.

"It was a nightmare. The merger boys not only attacked us for the way we were running the company, but they hired detectives to look into our private lives. We couldn't make a move without being sued by a stockholder. The better the company did, the more the sharks kept swimming around us. The worst part of their takeover strategy was they said they intended to buy *our* company with *our* cash. They also declared they would sell off our profitable subsidiaries to raise capital to retire *their* debt.

"The more they studied our assets the more they drooled all over their Wall Street Journals."

"I have to assume then that you took action."

"The only thing we could do was call in the bankers and lawyers to devise a shark repellent takeover defense.

"The first thing they did after examining all our books was criticize us for having one of the most outstanding management and profit records of any company in the United States. Based on our earnings they were amazed we hadn't been acquired before."

Cogswell continued, "It was hard to explain to them that our policy, since old man Dapperdan founded the company, has always been to have low debt, maintain high cash balances and give our stockholders a fair return on their money. They heard us out and then said we were not in tune with the times. The only way to save the company from a takeover was to make ourselves so unattractive that no one would go near us with a 10-foot junk bond."

"What shark repellent did they suggest?"

"For starters they made us unload our cash surplus by buying several companies that were worthless. After making the acquisitions they persuaded us to borrow as much money at high interest rates as the traffic would bear. They proved to us that the more debt we built up the more chance we had of surviving in the takeover jungle."

Cogswell went on, "It wasn't enough to have high indebtedness and no cash—we also had to produce low earnings so the stock would be overpriced on the market. Last year our shares looked like a dream buy. Now we're in the bottom of the tank."

I said, "You apparently followed your investment bankers' and lawyers' advice to the letter."

"It wasn't easy to turn the company overnight from a winner into a loser, but we managed to do it," he said proudly. "I can only take so much credit—my management team has to be given recognition for the precarious position the company now finds itself in."

"And although you're almost bankrupt you can still smile?"

"Why not? Thanks to our strategy no one has tried to take us over for six months."

of many top executives who do not share Pickens's amusement. Commenting on the negative effects of Unocal Oil's taking on $4 billion in debt to ward off the 1985 Pickens-led raid on his company, Hartley comments, "Every day we open the door [now] we spend $2 million for interest. Think what that would have done for the U.S. if it had been put into job creation." Putting such massive debt burdens on our corporations, adds Paul Christopherson, an analyst with Bear, Sterns & Company, also "means you let people go, which reduces employment, and you cut back on capital spending, which reduces economic growth, and you cut discretionary spending, like research, which has long-term implications."

Many Fortune 500 companies are being told by Wall Street that they have no significant reason to exist, not because their products are unpopular or selling poorly, but because speculators and other investors can get a higher quick return if these companies dismantle themselves by selling off divisions, merging, or otherwise restructuring. Institutional investors, accounting for eight out of every ten trades on the major stock exchanges, "are traders, not investors," says George Keller, chairman of Chevron, adding that they "have all the principles of a dog in heat."

There is hardly a large corporation left in America that is untouched by the decade's epidemic of restructurings. The amount of money spent in search of higher share price is staggering. Net long-term debt taken on by nonfinancial corporations nearly quadrupled between 1983 and 1987, starting at $40 billion and skyrocketing to close to $160 billion. In 1986 alone, 4,000 companies spent nearly $200 billion on stock buybacks and other restructuring efforts. In 1985, the dollar value of mergers, acquisitions, divestitures, buyouts, and other deals soared 169 percent and equaled the total assets of GM, Exxon, Mobil, and ITT combined. Stockbrokers were delighted. "'About one-third of the gain in the Standard & Poor's Corp. index of 500 stocks [that year] came from stock prices bolstered by restructuring,' said Steve Einhorn, co-chairman of investment policy at Goldman Sachs & Co."

By 1987, investor incentives to demand more restructurings became even clearer and increased the pressure on companies that continued to resist them. As U.S. corporate debt went through the roof, the borrowing firms' profits and number of employees both declined. But Wall Street's demands were met; once restructured, these firms' share prices skyrocketed. This trend continues uninterrupted. "Investment bankers expect the merger business to continue at a torrid pace," financial writer Herb Greenberg reported, after Wall Street was rocked by insider trading scandals in late 1986. Contrary to expectation, these scandals have not reduced the pressures on American corporations to restructure, raise short-term profits and share price, lower costs, and cut payrolls.

Driving the frenzy of corporate executives to restructure is the bone-chilling fear that if they don't, their corporations are sitting ducks in a year-round hunting season. They know how easily large unrestructured companies with undervalued share prices can be attacked and gobbled up without warning, or forced to suddenly sell off divisions and fire employees within weeks. In 1986, many people rubbed their eyes in wonder as companies as large as Goodyear, RCA, Chesebrough-Pond's, Holiday Inn, Ex-Cell-O, Safeway, Gillette, Owens-Corning, Brooks Brothers, and Anderson-Clayton disappeared from the roster of independent firms or were forced into drastic restructurings to avoid being taken over.

When Ralston-Purina and Quaker competed for food giant Anderson, Clayton & Co., they sought just one prize from among the target firm's many products: its Gaines brand of dog food. After Quaker won, it kept the Gaines line and sold off the remaining brands owned by Anderson-Clayton. For investors, these deals are sweet, but for the managers of companies and divisions suddenly put "in play," yesterday's rules, promises, and plans to climb the company's career ladder are suddenly transformed into today's uncertainty and fear of firing.

Chesebrough-Pond's, the maker of chemical, food, and consumer products, began 1986 as number 136 on the Fortune 500. But that autumn, its board and top managers had to choose whether to dismantle the firm or support its sale to another company. When Chesebrough's investors got a surprise offer to sell its stock for a price higher than the shares were trading, Wall Street 's financial analysts announced that the company either had "to accept the American Brands bid or come up with a better alternative, such as arranging a friendly takeover or undergoing a restructuring." Its low share price and success at having resisted the pain of restructuring had limited the company's options severely. Chesebrough's executives became "all but resigned to the fact that the company would be acquired." And within days, the company was bought by the British giant Unilever.

In modern-day business versions of Greek tragedy, executives are leading the charge on their own companies. They carry out Wall Street's orders to restructure often before learning that their company is a target.

The increase in self-restructurings is an important ripple effect of the smaller number of highly publicized hostile takeovers. Most restructurings do not occur because the firm lost a takeover battle, or as the result of beating back a raider. Most restructurings occur because top executives pull the triggers on their own companies. A defensive strategy of "Downsize and Dismantle," of "raid yourself first and be safer," has taken hold. "We try to do what's best for the business, but we were casting an eye to the jungle of Wall Street," says Ruben Mettler, chief executive of TRW, about the 1986 restructuring of the nation's fifty-seventh largest company. "Knowing we were vulnerable" helped shape the asset sales, cutbacks, and higher debt piled on to the delight of stockholders, who saw the value of their shares rise as a result. When top executives put their own restructuring studies into motion to "save" the company from the possibly worse trauma of becoming a takeover casualty, they usually bring on the same terrors they hoped to prevent others from forcing on their company and its managers.

Investment bankers and respected business consultants are especially quick to advise any company lucky enough to have avoided a restructuring to ante up and enter its management, staff, and other assets in this fashionable high-stakes demolition derby. "I see a client and I say 'You're an ideal target for [raider] Victor Posner,'" says John Patience, a corporate strategy consultant at prestigious McKinsey & Company. Driving the point home, he reminds executives, "Management can do exactly the same things as the raiders." Why not just do it before they come after you? Jim Farley, senior chairman of Booz Allen & Hamilton, agrees, flatly stating, "If a chief executive officer isn't thinking of restructuring, he's not doing his job." Many chief executives still honestly claim that the motive for putting their companies through brutal restructurings is to *save* them from what would happen if a raider gained control of the firm. They fear that to conduct business in a time-honored prudent fashion, crazy as it seems, can too easily lead to the company's total destruction.

The late AMF's takeover experience is, very likely, one of the more scary alternatives weighing on their minds. Once known as American Machine and Foundry, AMF last reported sales of $1.1 billion. It was number 288 on Fortune's list of the 500 largest industrials in 1985. In July of that year, Irwin Jacobs announced that his firm, Minstar, had bought over 50 percent of AMF's stock.

Within six weeks, Mr. Jacobs—also known as "Irv the Liquidator"—put "For Sale" signs on units accounting for 53 percent of the corporation's total revenues. He reportedly "said he personally had fired" the company's chairman and president (both aged fifty-one) and that "only about 50" corporate-level employees would remain by year-end. Most of AMF's 400-member corporate staff was fired. "It was like a morgue around here before," said one employee who was just fired, referring to the month between the takeover and the layoffs, "now it's like a cemetery." Within days, *Business Week* estimated that by selling off thirteen AMF units, which he also described as "winners," Jacobs would recoup the entire $564 million purchase price for this hostile acquisition. This suggests he may have succeeded in acquiring the remaining 47 percent of AMF for almost no money at all.

Few chief executives taking their own companies through a restructuring would wield the ax as harshly as AMF's new boss.

Typically, they keep more of the company intact and follow a more gradual, less drastic interpretation of this sort of "asset management." But to accuse them, as raiders do, of restructuring only out of fear of losing their "entrenched" jobs, conveniently ignores two facts. First, long-term executives personally know and usually care more about the companies and people they lead than do the raiders and their backers, who have only looked at the company's numbers from afar. Second, of all the employees in the firm, top executives have the most lucrative exit contracts. Most also have far more pleasant job alternatives available than presiding over the destruction of the companies and careers they helped build. When top executives stick around to keep raiders from restructuring the company, or to minimize the chaos that follows if the company is merged or taken over, they have more praiseworthy noneconomic motives for staying than just keeping their salaries. Even though they usually fail in this effort, many stay on hoping that the restructuring they organize will result in less pain for their employees than would have followed in a hostile takeover.

Chief executive Robert E. Mercer's heroic efforts to save Goodyear in 1986 from raider James Goldsmith and his investment banker provide an eloquent example of this dilemma. In a candid letter to Goodyear's employees explaining what actions would be required to "save" the company from being torn apart by raiders, Mercer wrote, "It is necessary to sacrifice both our long-term plans and our current assets, to narrow our business focus and shorten the time frame for stock performance . . . By moving first, we hope to emerge with more of the company intact than if we simply left our fate to a group who might well dismember Goodyear with reckless abandon."

The effort to save Goodyear soon came to resemble what happened at Phillips Petroleum. To pacify large investors, Goodyear more than doubled its debt; dropped 4,000 employees, including researchers and managers at closed plants and headquarters; repurchased half of its own shares; sold off 25 percent of its assets;

and slashed its budgets for long-term investments in research, development, and capital spending. analysts, both inside and outside the company agreed that, without warning and practically overnight, the proud industry leader whom employees had counted on to keep growing into a bright future, had become unsure of itself, cash poor, depressed, and forced to emphasize short-term results.

The financial press soon reported "drastic cutbacks," "an acute need for cash," and "few prospects for growth as [Goodyear] abandons a long-range diversification plan and shrinks. . . ." Mr. Mercer told reporters that the experience "knocked us backward," took away "an important part of our future," and caused him to "start checking the stock price every day, sometimes several times a day. . . ."

If the self-restructuring at Goodyear, overseen by top executives seeking to minimize its negative impact on employees, was this painful, what is the lesson for managers? The urgent message is that you should be prepared at all times just in case! When the restructuring arrives unexpectedly, no one will ask if your parachute is packed and ready. But the lesson from managers at firms such as Goodyear, Phillips, and many more who have gone through it is that your job is already on the line.

Goodyear, "an admittedly boastful company that was able to put a $1 billion pipeline across the Southwest and plan ten years ahead of most competitors, [was instantly reduced to urging] its employees to retire and cut out much of its leading-edge research." When the thirty-fifth largest U.S. industrial corporation, with 135,000 employees worldwide, was powerless to protect its managers or itself from such a rapid and unwanted restructuring, its managers quickly learned that in business today you cannot simply assume good things will continue. You must learn to look out for yourself.

2. *Mergers, Acquisitions and Stock Buybacks: Red Alerts for Managers*

When you pay a big premium, you spend your time servicing the debt, not operating the company.

F. Ross Johnson, Chief Executive Officer
R. J. Reynolds Industries, Inc.,
recent acquirer of Nabisco, Del Monte,
Planters, and other brands

Since 1983, American corporations have forked over more than $200 billion to purchase each other. Like other restructurings, big mergers incur enormous debts and usually result in the new parent company selling assets and forcing out personnel just as if they had been acquired in a more hostile takeover. The standard reply when this happens is always something like "These are only hors d'oeuvres compared to the banquet raiders would have turned us into and served up at the next auction sale." Well, maybe.

"If Allegheny is a white knight, God save us from white knights," says a Sunbeam executive who retired a few months after the merger. "They were pretty heavy handed. They went at us with a meat ax." In fact, as organizational psychologist

Mitchell Marks notes, "there is no such thing as a white knight, only shades of gray." This observation was underscored in the title of Isadore Barmash's book on this subject: *Welcome to Our Conglomerate, You're Fired!*

It is the rare merger that overcomes the temptation or necessity to dismiss managers and squeeze the new acquisition for money to repay the new parent firm's delighted bankers. When you hear that a merger or acquisition is coming, the issue to ponder is not "Will there be any changes?" Of course there will. The questions to pose are "How many? How sweeping? How soon? And who will still be around to carry them out?"

Consider this fired manager's experience as reported by *Wall Street Journal* writer Lawrence Ingrassia: "Last fall Sherwin-Williams Co. cleaned house shortly after its white-knight acquisition of Gray Drug Stores Inc. During negotiations before the acquisition, a fired Gray Drug executive recalls, 'Sherwin-Williams indicated there would be few changes.' He adds, 'My boss was fired the day after the merger.'"

The burden of running and keeping the acquired organization together falls on its remaining managers. Not everyone will be invited to stay on, and depending on how warmly the new owners welcome the old team, many may not wish to remain. Key managers, including your boss, may leave before you. A chilling statistic to keep in mind, especially if the merger was not sought by the company's top managers, is the finding by executive recruiting firm Lamalie Associates that 52 percent of top management typically jump ship within three years after a takeover.

While a merger is taking place is the time for managers to start to think and act like free agents in case they may need to exercise their options later. "I remember hearing someone say, A merger has been committed against us," recalls Homer Hagedorn, a consultant with the Arthur D. Little Company. When you hear one may be on the way, ask yourself, "Who will be hit by the restructurings that are sure to follow?" As more reliable information becomes available, compare the two corporate cultures being joined, and find out how compatible they are. An important question is, How much freedom do people in the other company's operations have to make important decisions for their units? If the answer is "very little" and you are used to having a lot, expect problems.

After a merger, many companies announce that their number of employees has shrunk back to the parent company's size before the acquisition occurred. This feat of efficiency required another round of the by-now-familiar medicine of firings, sell-offs, and closings of units brought in by the consolidation. These usually come as an unexpected shock to the managers most affected, especially when the merger was described as "friendly," or the company was happily "rescued" by a white knight.

A number of service departments are likely candidates for consolidation. Especially vulnerable are audit and accounting groups, public relations and planning departments, data processing units, and corporate staff, for these positions are usually duplicated at the parent company. The higher the price paid for the company, and the larger the loans run up by the new parent, the more likely it is that jobs will be eliminated. These are especially likely when the new parent firm paid cash for the acquisition, rather than exchanging its stock for that of its new subsidiary.

The Fall of Gulf Oil

On March 6, 1984, Gulf Oil Corporation was acquired for $12 billion by Chevron Oil. News of Gulf's acquisition and subsequent dismantling stopped corporate executive and raider alike for a shared moment of awe and amazement. Chevron Chairman George Keller said he moved after it became clear "Gulf was a business that was about to be destroyed." Overnight, an unknown Oklahoman named T. Boone Pickens changed corporate history.

Before Gulf's desperate merger with Chevron, no company that large and powerful had ever been so defeated or even challenged by a corporate raider. Pickens inspired a whole new generation of raiders by demonstrating how easily raids could be conducted through careful planning, nerves of steel, and a few friends on Wall Street. When Gulf's board realized that the large institutions holding the company's shares would be perfectly happy to sell them to the highest bidder, it sought out a merger partner it believed would be less likely than Mr. Pickens to sell off large chunks of the company. In the end, Chevron offered a higher price and bought out Pickens's stake, instantly making him millions of dollars richer.

Gulf's managers, while sorry to see their company change hands, felt this outcome would preserve the company as they knew it. After all, they were merging with a like-minded player, "one of their own" in the industry still known as the world's most powerful private club. Chevron's executives did not approve of Pickens either, and most Gulf managers assumed that the two companies would join together and get back to being oilmen again.

The personal disasters that befell Gulf's employees after their company's "rescue" should come as no surprise when you consider that Chevron borrowed roughly $12 billion to purchase Gulf. With interest payments alone of $650 million a year, no one should expect to see their firm conducting business as usual. Within a year, nearly one-third of Gulf employees were gone. Joint work force reductions affected more than 16,000 people who were dismissed outright or removed from the payroll when their Gulf or Chevron units were auctioned after the merger. Twelve thousand additional employees from both companies were offered sweetened early retirement packages if they would leave immediately.

The impact of Gulf's sale on its managers was summed up by *US News & World Report* a year later:

> No matter how they fared, Gulf employees agree that the merger disrupted lives, uprooted families, altered career paths, and wrecked personal budgets. [For] Charles Rhoads . . . leaving Gulf after 16 years was traumatic. "You have all the Gulf T-shirts and cuff links," he explains. "It is more than a job. It's part of your life."

Gulf's vice president for industrial relations defended the work force reductions, saying, "What's happening here is a Sunday school picnic compared to what it would have been like" had Pickens taken possession of the company. Maybe so, but for managers fired in a debt-ridden restructuring, the difference between a friendly merger and a hostile takeover hardly matters. For many, the only difference between them is simply who pulls the trigger. The human toll remains extraordinary.

In addition to the disrupted lives of thousands of discharged workers, many employees who were not terminated were transferred, and now wake up in a different city, report to a different boss, and worry about working at a new parent company whose culture is light-years away from what they had always taken for granted at Gulf. Consider these telling examples from an early *Wall Street Journal* report:

- Accustomed to liberal perks and broad authority, (Gulf managers) are finding Chevron a lean, centrally run company where top management reviews even small decisions. They wonder if they will fit in at Chevron, whose "executives talk more like economists than good ole boys," and whose "legendary clannishness" may block promotions for Gulf refugees.
- These executives chiefly fear that they won't get much autonomy in the Chevron system

> . . . For example, a Gulf oil trader was dismayed when a Chevron trader asked which Gulf supervisor approved his trades. "I do my trades without approval," he told the Chevron employee who, in turn, was stunned by the answer. Another Gulf employee says . . . "Whenever I want to initiate a project at Gulf, I just go ahead and do it. But at Chevron, they seem to take titles and structures very seriously."
>
> - They also worry about moving from Houston or Pittsburgh to San Francisco, "a city that many of them consider weird." They are nervous about relocating there and calling it their new home. . . . "Tension at Gulf is prompting a bit of gallows humor." From one executive: "Only half my associates are worried that they won't get an offer at Chevron. The other half are worried that they will."

After Chevron's restructuring, there are few reminders that Gulf ever existed. What was previously the nation's fifth largest oil company has totally disappeared from Pittsburgh, its headquarters city, and seen its operations base in Houston downsized 50 percent. Over half the employees invited to relocate from Pittsburgh to San Francisco refused to join Chevron there. Gulf properties that were sold off include refineries in Philadelphia and Puerto Rico, over 5,000 gas stations on the East Coast, and its Canadian operations. The name "Gulf" has disappeared from the letterhead of the combined companies.

Chevron's management worked hard to minimize the emotional stress, income loss, and other painful disruptions experienced by its employees. This is no easy task. The best that acquiring firms can hope to accomplish is to protect as many able managers as possible from being sacrificed in the chaos that follows. In these trade-offs, there is no way for top management to protect every valued employee.

There is good reason to question whether these restructurings, retrenchments, and massive dislocations are worth their human and financial costs. For Wall Street investors, they are worth their weight in gold. T. Boone Pickens almost single-handedly drove up Gulf's share price from $35 to $80 in less than eight months. He opened the door to the many more takeovers and restructurings that followed, and became a cult hero after the fall of Gulf. Pickens and his associates cleared a gross profit of $760 million when they sold Chevron their shares in Gulf. They received $1.70 back for every dollar they had invested only a few months before. Sixty-five million dollars in fees went to Merrill Lynch, Salomon Brothers, and First Boston, just three of the Wall Street firms representing companies involved in Gulf's demise. Arbitrageurs, professional speculators in takeover stocks, cleared $300 million on Gulf's rising share price. Mayor Edward Koch joined in Wall Street's celebration party and toasted Pickens for bringing $50 million in additional billings for the New York law firms representing all sides of just this one battle for corporate control.

"In New York today, two conglomerates gobbled each other up and disappeared without a trace."

Jubilation reigned at investment and law offices all over Wall Street because enormous fees follow takeover battles and restructurings regardless of which side wins. At the time, Gulf's sale price of $13.3 billion broke all records for the amount spent on an acquisition. Wall Street bankers anticipated that even bigger mergers and takeovers were sure to follow. Indeed, Gulf's fall brought in so much new business that it was only a short time before the merger and acquisition units of Wall Street's investment banks became the most profitable of all their departments.

Few managers and workers at merged or acquired companies have reason to share in these celebrations. Pickens's $760 million gross profit from the sale of Gulf Oil amounted to $65,000 for each one of the first 12,000 people to be fired from the company. While Pickens did not fire anyone himself, and I am sure that he bears these employees no ill will, the message to managers throughout corporate America is loud and clear: "Your job is at risk. No matter how good you are or how long you've been there, working for big companies no longer means money, glamour, and job security until you retire."

At the executive level, Gulf's flight from corporate raiders into a friendlier merger with Chevron will be remembered as the most chilling business event of the 1980s. Even though it was only the first of many, no one had ever seen anything like this happen before. The unmistakable message to all vulnerable managers was that if the fourteenth largest corporation in America could be downed so easily, there's no reason why your company couldn't be next. *Business Week* reported growing concerns that Gulf's "painful defeat has left observers gasping at how swiftly a giant can be bagged." When powerful Gulf Oil could not marshal Wall Street support to beat back a little-known "big-hat boy" from Oklahoma, top managers realized that no company was safe from restructurings and shotgun mergers.

Stock Buybacks: Abandoning the Future

The world of corporate finance is unrelated to the real world of goods and services. Instead of generating new wealth, corporations are playing a giant game of asset rearrangement that is largely unproductive.

Professor Robert Reich
Harvard University

The practice of companies "investing" corporate funds to purchase their own shares at the stock market has reached epidemic proportions during the 1980s. By reducing the number of its shares circulating, any company can engineer higher share prices. If it spends enough money buying itself, the steep share price rise delights short-term investors and sends possible raiders looking elsewhere for lower-priced bargains. With shareholders happy and raiders deterred, a company should be able to stop looking over its shoulder, run its own businesses, and become a safer and more attractive place to work, or so the theory goes.

The idea of stock buybacks is attractive until one asks where all the money came from for these purchases. Large buybacks mean an enormous outflow of capital that otherwise could have been used to grow and position the company for the future. But "few companies risk tempting a raider by holding a big wad of cash. And many find it prudent to return capital to shareholders instead of investing in new ventures that might take years to turn profitable," notes *Wall Street Journal* reporter Ralph Winter. In order to buy back millions of their own shares, companies raid their own treasuries and then borrow incredible amounts more to finance the rest. Their executives must then decide which key employees to force out, and which units to close down or sell off so the company can report "savings" and pay off the mounting costs of its borrowing binge. For everyone remaining, it can mean budget cuts rather than expanding opportunities, and fewer management positions likely to provide visibility.

Since 1984, corporate debt has skyrocketed to heights most prudent boards and executives would veto if they were still able to manage their companies with an eye to the future. Imagine the difference an extra $100 billion would have made to America's largest corporations over the last few years. Corporations spent more than $100 *billion* just buying their own shares back from the stock market during the three years ending January 1987. This is in addition to the billions more spent to acquire other companies. One hundred billion is more money than most governments spend in a year. All of the oil imported into the United States in 1986 cost only half that much. This is an unbelievably wasteful expenditure for insurance protection against takeovers.

The billions of dollars siphoned from these corporations is money that could have contributed to expanding business opportunities for the organization and its employees and permitting a variety of other expenditures traditionally associated with corporate citizenship. Instead, top executives in dozens of corporations will spend years explaining to managers and workers why there will be no more expansion, interesting promotions, better job assignments, or raises. Any group spending $100 billion in three years is bound to come up too short to go after the same business opportunities they would have jumped at earlier, when they still had one or two of those billions on hand.

Whenever companies announce a major buyback of their own shares, it is time for managers to dig good foxholes and begin to think like free agents. Business units that seemed integral to the firm yesterday will show up on the auction block tomorrow. In your future opportunities, you should anticipate that the firm will cut back on the number of markets and lines of business it is pursuing. If your sponsor is over fifty, expect to lose him to the early retirement program. Keep in mind that although top executives resent having to shovel out so much of the company's money and personnel, investors love the effects of downsizing and dismantling. Investors will cheer chief executives as brave statesmen and applaud the company's rising share price. But remember, it could be your job and your unit whose liquidation they are celebrating.

CBS on the Ropes

Takeovers and restructurings come to each industry in waves. When TWA disappeared into Carl Icahn's empire, other airlines took protective measures to become less attractive to raiders. Broadcasting companies experienced their first wave of destruction in 1985, when Wall Street put all three major television networks (or their then-parent corporations) "in play."

Within a year, it was all over. Both NBC and ABC were quickly acquired by new owners. CBS responded to its takeover threat by undertaking a stock buyback, which led to more drama than any six of its soap operas and crime shows combined. As one would expect, within months after the restructurings, employment was cut and morale plunged at all three once-glamorous television showcases.

The troubles at CBS, for years the most powerful, most profitable, and best-managed of the three networks, began when entrepreneur Ted Turner, backed by junk bonds from investment bank Drexel Burnham, sought to take over the company. He was quickly joined by "just about every widely known corporate raider except J. R. Ewing of 'Dallas.'" Few of them showed any interest in building on the company's reputation for high-quality news and entertainment, but all could see profitable ways to dismantle the corporation.

Turner outraged William Paley, CBS's founder and former chairman, when he suggested he would recoup much of the purchase price by simply selling off CBS's Columbia records, publishing, and other subsidiaries. Paley replied that they were not separate properties, but rather mutually reinforce one another; that CBS's "strength and health are the products of more than a half century of careful, concerned nurturing by a great many dedicated people. To risk its loss would be to trifle recklessly with the company's future and with the public interest."

CBS management clearly disagreed with Wall Street's "cash cow" view that this was a company to be chopped up and sold off piece by piece to the highest bidders. Once "in play," however, the value of the company's stock skyrocketed. Notorious arbitrageur Ivan Boesky and other Wall Street speculators made millions on the jumps in CBS's share price. While CBS responded quickly to the threat, it was at a high cost to its employees and its own future financial security. In July 1985, the company more than doubled its debt load to buy back 21 percent of its own shares, at an inflated, speculators' "takeover" price greater than twice the price it had been just six months earlier. The cost was $1 billion in funds CBS otherwise might have spent on its own business.

The managerial cost at CBS from this unexpected raid on its corporate treasury was disastrous. Within weeks, 2,000 long-term employees were offered a one-time-only early retirement "opportunity" to give up their jobs and disappear. If everyone eligible took advantage of the offer, the company's work force would have sustained a 7 percent drop. Executives made it clear that other cost-cutting programs were sure to follow, and their severity would be influenced by the number of older employees taking early retirement.

Companies often reinforce this type of subtle pressure to leave with the implicit message that if you remain, your job will have little meaning and carry even less weight. It will be a "red circle," aptly defined by one close observer as a "dead-end position offered chiefly to protect employers against age-discrimination suits. Entailing no paycut, they promise scant chance of a raise anytime in the 20th century."

Thirty percent of CBS's managers aged fifty-five or older took immediate early retirement. Firings then began in earnest. In 1986, over 1,000 positions were "eliminated." After 700 were fired in a single month, one official said, "There exists a degree of corporate insecurity at CBS the likes of which I've never seen before." Most visibly angered were the reporters and staff in CBS's news division. Among the first to go were seventy-four fired professionals, including veteran correspondents Liz Trotta and George Herman, who were reportedly given only two days to clear out their desks. The disgruntled executive producer of "60 Minutes," Don Hewitt, created a stir by offering to buy the entire news division. Reacting to CBS's plans to sell off at least $300 million in assets to pay for its stock buyback, Hewitt recruited Dan Rather, Mike Wallace, and Bill Moyers, among others, and said, "If they're going to sell CBS News, why not to us? We love it, it's our baby, and . . . we wanted right of first refusal."

Shortly afterward, CBS's chief executive Thomas Wyman promised no more "surprises" or "dramatic news." He downplayed the prospect of more group firings, and credited the large exodus of managers taking early retirement with saving others' jobs at the company. Then, in September 1986, Wyman was fired by the CBS board for soliciting offers from other companies to buy the firm. Laurence Tisch, the "white squire" who had earlier purchased nearly 25 percent of CBS shares and "rescued" the firm from additional takeover threats, was named CBS's new chief. Mr. Tisch, a highly successful executive in the fields of insurance, hotels, tobacco, and other businesses, had no previous experience in broadcasting.

During Tisch's first month at the helm, *Fortune* reported industry sources predicting CBS would soon eliminate over 1,000 additional jobs. According to one report from the new corporate war zone, "A CBS executive says Tisch recently asked him to explain his role at the company. Tisch listened for a time, then asked how many people worked for him. 'Twelve,' the executive said. 'Pick your best person,' Tisch replied, 'and get rid of the rest.'"

In March 1987, soon after selling off its publishing division, CBS announced another $30 million in firings and other "savings" in its news division. Dan Rather and Diane Sawyer offered to take salary cuts to save the jobs of some of the 215 newly fired CBS News employees. They joined Mike Wallace and other picketers protesting cuts in jobs and benefits outside CBS headquarters. *New York Times* columnist Russell Baker commented acidly, "Mr. Tisch is a hotel man. Chambermaids don't kid themselves. He must have thought news people were at least as smart." Echoing the bitterness of displaced managers in other industries as well, fired long-time correspondent Ike Pappas said, "The quality, integrity, and standards we had are being compromised by [the] accountants. . . ."

Shortly after this round of cuts, Mr. Tisch stated, "News is a public trust first and I take this very seriously. But, by the same token, it is also a business." "To launch a public relations effort on the network's behalf," Tisch also hired an outside advisor, having earlier fired much of CBS's own corporate public relations staff.

Even though CBS, like Goodyear and Phillips Petroleum, was "victorious" and stayed independent, managers at the company paid dearly for that independence. For most employees, it is nearly impossible to distinguish between the painful self-restructuring undertaken by the company's chief executives and the restructuring a raider would have done. Each company has gone through a wrenching downsizing, paid off its raiders and short-term shareholders, and remains little more than a fond memory for managers who knew it before Wall Street's attack. All three companies were respected leaders in their industries. Each was well managed, and harshly penalized for its excellence. While all three paid the ransom to remain independent, not one is the same company to work for that it was before the financial powers-that-be went after it.

For those managers still on board, each company must demonstrate that there are still opportunities for advancement and challenging career moves within the remaining divisions. In rough situations like these, managers are well advised to know their alternatives and prepare in advance as soon as they see trouble coming. Massive buybacks can cripple a company as badly as being taken over. Once again, managers must not wait until they know if their company "won" the battle or not. Either way, their jobs are on the line.

Winners and Losers in Takeovers and Restructurings

The biggest winners from takeovers, stock buybacks, and shotgun mergers are professional speculators, financial organizations, and institutional investors. By successfully milking companies as if they were cash cows and restricting their growth to nothing more long-term than next quarter's cash flow, these investors emerge greatly enriched, and for the present as the victorious force with which managers must now reckon.

The biggest losers in the merger and takeover wars are the companies, their employees, and the shared values of loyalty, rewards for performance, and commitment. Managers are responding to the harsh impact of restructuring cutbacks by cutting back their own devotion, commitment, and loyalty to their companies. Managers are more likely to answer calls from headhunters and walk out as soon as better opportunities beckon than to keep going the extra mile for "the company" that may not be there tomorrow. Free Agent Managers know they are working in a chancy corporate world, where a good company can be cashiered as fast as a bad one by Wall Street whenever the company's "breakup value" is higher than its current share price.

What such extreme, short-term financial strategies ignore, of course, is that loyalty is not a one-way street. The decline of loyalty will continue because nobody likes to be "had." More and more managers are finding they can no longer rely on their companies to provide the security and promotions anticipated as a reward for high performance. And as companies increasingly discourage long service and loyalty in their employees, more managers will decide they cannot afford to be the "world's last nice guy." "Downsizing is a short-term way of raising cash," notes *Business Week,* but "corporate loyalty may soon be as passé in the U.S. as investing in heavy equipment" if the cash cow perspective continues to operate in company after company.

Noticeable drops in company loyalty should not be surprising in light of the nastier corporate cultures forced on companies by financial wizards who have essentially written loyalty off. In an increasingly tense and uncertain corporate world, more managers will pack their own parachutes by adopting new career-building strategies developed precisely to help them learn how to defend themselves in an increasingly hostile environment.

The concept of free agentry is designed to protect managers from falling into the trap of giving a loyalty that is not returned. Understanding what it means to act as a free agent helps managers to gain control over their own fate. Organizational psychologist Robert Sutton has shown that after people have taken measures to protect themselves, "any given source of distress," such as panic and fears about job loss, "will cause less psychological and physical harm." The free agent concept is designed to increase self-confidence and minimize anxiety over job changes. For example, considering other job offers at a time when you *don't* need one is a constructive activity; it stimulates your imagination and gives you practice at applying for attractive alternatives to your current job, all under nonpanic conditions. Managers who act like free agents can gain important psychological and career-building benefits from their newly acquired openness toward increased mobility, higher salaries, and improved job opportunities.

Takeovers and restructurings are also reducing loyalty ties between corporations and the communities in which they do business. As citizens in cities as diverse as Findley, Ohio; Bartlesville, Oklahoma; Pittsburgh, Pennsylvania; and Danville, Virginia, have shown, the lives of communities revolve around their local industries. Thousands of lives are threatened when new or potential owners in far-away offices announce that the company will be moved and its "hometown" plants and offices closed. "One of the negatives that has come out of the dramatic restructuring of American business . . . [is that for the new crop of top managers] it becomes positively un-American to look at anything except their bottom line," says William S. Woodside, former chief executive of American Can Co. Under this pressure, total corporate giving to nonprofit organizations engaged in social services, education, or the arts fell off in 1986 for the first time in fifteen years, reports the Conference Board, a business research organization.

For local officials, the new short-run cash cow policies can mean broken promises. Perhaps the community has just floated a $40 million bond to build an industrial park to subsidize the company's new plant or warehousing facility. Community commitment to reduce utility rates and lower taxes also may have helped to subsidize the new operation. When new management suddenly moves the company out, then the entire city, just like the corporation's own work force, cannot avoid feeling they've been "had."

Yonkers, New York, is just one of hundreds of cities concerned about how to deal with "good neighbor" corporations in a world of takeovers and restructurings. After the Otis Elevator Corporation lost its fight to remain independent, it soon became clear that long-standing ties between the company and the city were about to be broken. When United Technologies took over Otis in 1982, a century-long relationship based on mutual trust, traditional goodwill, and a handshake was destroyed. Otis had been based in Yonkers since 1853, but after the takeover, United Technologies announced Otis would leave Yonkers. The recently opened Otis plant, built on land bought with public money and employing 1,800 workers, was shut down. The city's mayor, naturally concerned about the community impact of the surprise relocation, was indignant about the decision and still told interviewers three years later of the city's "rape" and "absolute betrayal" by the company's takeover and disappearance.

Milwaukee and Pittsburgh are two larger cities still recovering from the loss of company shutdowns after takeovers or restructurings. Famous manufacturers of beer, such as Schlitz ("The Beer That Made Milwaukee Famous"), have been acquired and are now headquartered elsewhere. Milwaukee's well-known breweries are largely shuttered and the city's employment is down.

Pittsburgh, which feared losing USX to Carl Icahn, also was Gulf Oil's worldwide headquarters before the remnant of that corporation was moved to California. As the third largest home base for American companies, after New York and Chicago, Pittsburgh has seen its share of corporate victories and losses. Nevertheless, Gulf's sudden departure—as civic contributor, major employer, symbol of power—left a big gap in the city's culture, economy, and self-esteem. Pittsburgh's not-for-profit sector misses the generous donations from Gulf Corporation and its employees. Gulf's donations to United Way amounted to $700,000 in 1983, when the firm's total giving to local organizations topped $2 million. Civic organizations that lost money and volunteer support on account of Gulf's sale include hospitals, colleges, museums, and the world-renowned Pittsburgh Symphony.

More generally, the city misses the $75 million that Gulf's payroll pumped into the economy every year. Pittsburgh's shock at losing Gulf was best described by the *Wall Street Journal* right after the company's sale was announced:

> Gulf Corp. shareholders may be smiling, but this city isn't . . . Mayor Richard Caliguiri says he is "furious" with T. Boone Pickens, Jr. . . . Mr. Caliguiri shouts, "I wish there was something I could do to make Pickens invest [his] three-quarters of a billion [gross profit from the merger] right here in Pittsburgh."

It is not yet clear whether the restructuring of American corporations is benefiting anyone besides investment bankers and their clients. As the United States moves closer to becoming a service economy rather than one rooted in manufacturing, some downsizings and consolidations seem unavoidable. At the same time, however, a multitude of reasonable questions arise concerning the long-term effects of the unusually harsh and lightning-quick manner in which these always-painful changes are being carried out. Free Agent Managers are becoming more realistic and less devoted to any one company, but it is unlikely that American business can develop a new generation of managers in this climate who can meet the challenges of the twenty-first century.

Two economists who have their doubts are Pat Choate, author of *The High-Flex Society,* and Robert Eisner, a professor at Northwestern University. Choate sees America's mad dash to restructure as *reducing* our flexibility to respond to competitive challenges. Executives in the United States are "too busy fighting Wall Street to fight Japan," he says, concerned that the pressures this creates for short-term performance will leave us even less prepared to meet future challenges. Eisner, addressing the claim that restructurings create more wealth for Americans by producing higher stock prices, asks, "How can anyone say the market's rise is great for consumption when the gain is predicated on takeovers that usually result in laying off thousands of workers?"

Firings and layoffs now extend all the way up the corporate ladder. By 1987, nearly 50 percent of all surveyed in the Harris–*Business Week* poll of managers at America's 1,000 largest companies expected their employer to "cut back its salaried work force in the next few years." They saw no more connections between how well they did their job and how secure their job is in the company. This pessimistic outlook is supported by dismal predictions like *Fortune*'s observation that "whole layers of middle management [are about to be driven into] oblivion." Everyone seems to think this can happen only to others, but not to themselves. In chapter 3, we will meet ex-managers who discovered the hard way how easily it can happen to anyone.

3. When It Happens To You

I knew there were going to be cuts in my division, but I didn't think I'd be among them.

People kept telling me, "You're not being fired but your job no longer exists."

I was actually in love with a company once.

three fired managers, talking in 1985

Told of a worker who had been laid off after having given 30 years to his company, Pickens snapped, "Given? Didn't he get paid?"

Time, March 4, 1985

I put thirty-four years into this firm, Howard, and now I can't pay my insurance! You can't eat the orange and throw the peel away—a man is not a piece of fruit!

Willie Loman, in Act II of Arthur Miller's *Death of a Salesman*

Getting Fired

American corporations have fired nearly one million managers from their payrolls since 1980. These individuals have been kicked out and "surplussed," while millions more have watched helplessly as their friends and associates were invited to leave or summarily thrown out the door. Listen as some managers describe the pain and shock of being fired, or of watching friends try to recover from their very last meeting with the boss.

William Fairchild, a senior engineer, was fired in 1985 when Arco Petroleum closed the research facility where he worked. The company also shut down or sold off its operations in the eastern third of the country, fired 12,000 employees, and spent $4 billion (from these "savings" and new loans) to repurchase its own stock, possibly to avoid a hostile takeover.

We spoke on Fairchild's first day of unemployment.

> I had ten harrowing minutes of pure agony when I realized this was really it. We didn't hear they would dump everything east of the Mississippi till the day it came out in the newspaper. No one believed this could really happen, not till all 400 of us had to get out. It was an awfully strange feeling. Like the death of a relative—not really real until *after* the funeral. I know I won't see these people again, and they are some of my best friends. We all worked so well together and are now simply disappearing. Everyone is going to scatter. We're all scrambling, so people are bound to wind up all over the place.
>
> Yesterday I had to pack up my office for the very last time. This Tech Center has been my home away from home ever since I arrived seven years ago. Now it is closed. I feel very strange. Maybe you come to grips with it afterwards. When I remembered some files I wanted to bring over to engineering, they wouldn't let me back in! That didn't make sense from the human standpoint. If anyone had wanted to take the files they'd already had two months to walk out with them.
>
> Even after they announced Arco was leaving the East and Midwest, we thought the Tech Center would just move west, from Harvey, Illinois. No one thought it could really be totally shuttered. We have a fantastic reputation and track record.

The whole industry says we're a dynamite operation. We just assumed they'd want to keep us. Some are being offered transfers to LA, but final offers and acceptances aren't sorted out yet. Even though we're all unemployed right now, my poor manager has been worrying more about how we'll make out than about his own (un)employment. Other high-ranking guys have also turned down transfers and are now unemployed. They'll probably have more trouble finding new work than many who are younger and not as high up.

Our strong reputation is helping get jobs with other companies. But it makes you stop and think to watch the ones who were most loyal, who have been here the longest. They know the product side of the business and this company inside out. They have worked here over twenty years and they put so much of themselves into it, they now have no other place to go. One of the best is scared stiff. His kids are going off to college. He's lucky his house here is secured, but its value is lower than what it will cost to buy in most other places. He's taking a big fall.

My own priorities changed after the announcement. I'm not going to put work so far ahead of my personal life anymore. For one thing, I see how little anyone is valued for their contribution by big companies. I'm less willing now to always place work above doing things for myself, or taking advanced courses in school for my own skills.

Before, work always came first. I put off my other interests, saying they could just wait till things got slower. Well, they're certainly slower now. Did you see the *Wall Street Journal* on how managers are changing because companies can't be trusted anymore? It's not worth hanging around here. My talents and commitments weren't appreciated. In fact, for me to take a transfer now they'll have to offer much more

> than I would have asked before they wiped out so much of the company.

Fairchild's pain and disbelief are common reactions to being fired. Fear and uncertainty about if and where you'll be working reach epidemic proportions during mergers and downsizings. "Two weeks can make an enormous difference," says Fairchild. "They may be thinking it over. But why, if I'm good, are they taking so long?" Bill Fairchild was angry and scared by his unexpected firing.

Some managers must live through *months* of uncertainty while their confused top managements sort things out. Getting fired or held back in a restructuring has practically no relation to a manager's competence or performance on the job. Decisions to sell off business units or to cut positions and personnel in yet another round of retrenchment follow more from financial thinking than departmental politics.

The suddenness and shock of firings is a universal theme among employees. Marilee Prescott's description of her termination is not unusual:

> It was astonishing. A new vice president was sent in, gave my boss six days to get out, and fired me before we had exchanged ten words. I counted them. The ax fell when the company "reorganized." We had just assumed all along we'd be consulted more about decisions made, rather than treated with such a heavy hand. If we had failed in the marketplace it would have been easier to understand. But our products were performing very well. We were the second-largest-selling brand in the country.

Unlike William Fairchild, Marilee Prescott did not find another job within weeks of being fired. She joined the more than 30 percent of unemployed managers who remain without new positions for seven months or longer. By that time, even executives earning $50,000 a year or more exhaust severance pay averaging one week for each year with the company. One manager facing this problem was Kenneth King, a human resources director fired in 1985 when his employer was acquired. *Fortune*'s Felix Kessler reported that King's termination pay was running out. "Faced with uncertainty, he isn't replacing his 1977 Buick and is trying to talk his 17-year-old son into attending a local community college, rather than a private university as his older brother and sister did. . . . 'I try not to be bitter, but this has had an impact on my family and my career.'"

Kessler notes: "For many executives, the emotional cost of unexpectedly losing a job is more painful than the financial damage." Feelings of anger and betrayal are expressed by two managers fired by J. I. Case, in Wisconsin:

> "I was a dedicated employee," says Nick Kadamian, 44, former long-range planning manager . . . [and] a 21-year employee . . . "I worked weekends and stayed inside the plant to protect it during strikes." No matter. Kadamian, still jobless, is bitter. "I perceived my life as being part of the company," he says. "That's what hurts. I never perceived not retiring from there . . ." [Firings] can come when least expected. Jerome Metz, a former J. I. Case manager, had just received a solid raise and one of the highest performance evaluations in his 11-year career when he was terminated last November.

Being fired unexpectedly leaves wounds that last way beyond fears about a serious loss of income. The experience is personally degrading under any circumstance, but when the firing is abrupt and unrelated to the quality of a manager's performance on the job, it is especially crushing and humiliating. Grace Keaton held a responsible management position at a well-known publishing company. After twelve years with the firm, her position was eliminated when she was fired without warning. Listen to the pain Keaton describes to oral historian Harry Maurer:

Nothing led up to it. It was almost a total shock, with the exception of a few days beforehand, when I was just feeling something funny and dreadful. I couldn't even tell you what. I would see two people together in a place that was unusual to see them together. That kind of thing. But I had an appointment with my boss at 10:30 one morning and I came in with my pile of work, and I said, "Do you want me to begin with this contract?" And he said something like: "No, I want to begin by talking about your leaving this company." This company I had been with for twelve years. I didn't die, but I can't tell you why not.

Moreover, this was a man I had been almost nauseatingly loyal to, and I *felt* loyal to . . . In any case, it was total shock. I guess my mouth hung open for thirty seconds or so, and I said, brilliantly, "What do you mean? What do you mean?" But he had just said in no uncertain terms, "You are fired." And I said, "What do you mean? What do you mean?" And then I said, "Why? Why? Why? Why? Why?" He had all his speeches prepared, and I didn't, so his were shorter and evasive. He said it was all done. There was no going back. It was all signed, and the separation agreements were to his mind very generous. And there was no changing anything, and that was the way it was, and he was not about to give me any good reasons for this. Or any reasons . . . I was supposed to ask him questions. So I said, "Well, is it this? Is it that? Is it this? What is it?" He said, "Yes, sort of, well, no, well . . ." He just didn't want to talk about it. He wanted me to disappear. He just wanted me to drop out of the earth. You know, I probably should have clammed up and said, "I want to call my lawyer. . . ."

They had eliminated my job. And they have technically not replaced me . . . I felt completely betrayed . . . This had apparently been going on for quite a while. There was every opportunity to say to me, "This is going to happen; get out and look for a job." In fact, I had turned down a job. And other things had come up that I hadn't investigated because I thought, "Oh, you know, what the hell. They've changed the pension law, and I'm going to be fully vested soon. And there are things about this job that are attractive, and maybe the people who are running the [parent] corporation will decide to retire to Tahiti and some good people will come in." You know, that sort of indecisive thing you do. So I was absolutely devastated.

It was the worst blow I ever had. I've been divorced. My father died a few months before I got fired . . . I've been through a lot of emotional upheaval in my life, and I've never been through anything like getting fired. Never. It's funny—for a long time the first thing I asked everybody was "Have you ever been fired?" Because I had the feeling that they could not possibly understand anything I was going to say unless they had been. And for a while that was true. I was persuaded that I must be not only as bad as the company must have thought to fire me, but much worse than that. Probably the world's worst. Probably I didn't deserve to live. It doesn't simply take away your self-confidence. It destroys you. Utterly.

The amazing thing is that I have had this same thing described to me by people who were fired where they just cut out a department or closed a plant. They say the same thing. There is something in the act. I suppose there is something in our faith in and attitude towards work that says if you work well, you're going to be rewarded. That this is one of the virtues of our society . . . That there is something healthy, to use an old-fashioned word, about working well. So that if you're going to approach justice, that's where you're going to approach it. "Good people always get jobs." How many times have you heard that? . . . It's not true. But still, we believe it—and it's devastating, therefore, to be fired. I have still not recovered from it. I have had three job offers since then. Those offers have made no dent in that part of me that feels destroyed.

I must say my spirits were kept up by friends in the industry who called. A lot of people called. I owe a million deep-felt thank-you notes. They helped me look for another job. Somebody directed me to the unemployment office. Everyone who'd ever lost a job called up and said something nice. I think that probably got me through. I felt I had not been completely abandoned by everybody, that not everybody would be willing to betray me in the same way. The feelings were so elemental, and so strong, just overpowering. Betrayal. Depression. Shock. . . .

You know, you remember emotional experiences, and at some point you say, "I cannot summon up that experience anymore." It's just too long ago, or it wasn't strong enough. I can't imagine that happening with being fired. I think till I die, I will be able to summon it up again like dehydrated horror. If I just sprinkle a few drops of water on it, I will be able to summon up that first numb horror, rage, and the depression afterwards. Just total wipeout.

The Stress Caused by Firings

Grace Keaton is not alone in her feelings and experience. Anyone ever fired from a job he or she values has shared in the scary emotional devastation she so vividly describes. Being forced off the job makes people feel powerless, unable to predict what will happen next, and out of control. The heart, body, and mind all respond to these severe jolts with their own symptoms. Grace Keaton's grieving and distress are normal reactions to the shock of an unexpected firing. Other typical reactions seen by medical experts include sleep loss, depression, digestive problems, back trouble, higher blood pressure (hypertension), respiratory problems, and rising cholesterol levels. Already under pressure, fired people are prone to ignore or deny any of these common stress symptoms. Physicians consulted by fired employees also report less commonly occurring stress reactions that include higher incidences of arthritis, diabetes, ulcers, gout, and thyroid gland malfunctions.

The grief, anger, and humiliation experienced by fired managers is well known to anyone who has ever been through this shattering experience. It is summed up most eloquently by Harry Maurer in *Not Working:*

> Unemployed people have been robbed of something, and they know it. The bewilderment they often express is like that of the homeowner who returns to find rooms ransacked, valuable and beloved objects missing. The sense of violence and invasion, the feelings of fear and loss and helplessness, descend with the same stunning force when a worker is deprived of work. And the loss is much greater, because work, if the longing of the unemployed is any indication, remains a fundamental human need . . . It provides not simply a livelihood, but an essential passage into the human community. It makes us less alone.

Studies show, ironically, that the managers who are hurt worst in any firing are those who believe most strongly in the work ethic so prized by employers. Managers who personally identify most closely with their jobs and companies also suffer the worst stress when their positions are eliminated. The self-esteem of the people who take the most pride in their work suffers greatly when they are fired. Mistakenly, they often blame themselves.

Most fired managers report feelings of anger, betrayal, and rejection. Many are also overcome with self-blame. After speaking with dozens of fired people, Maurer notes that many, like Grace Keaton, insisted on taking the blame for being terminated. "What astonished me more than any other discovery was the degree to which unemployed people blame themselves." Coupled with this often undeserved guilt, the fear and depression from feeling isolated and abandoned can bring on even worse symptoms and consequences.

The most extreme reaction, of course, is when the fired manager or worker dies, soon after losing his or her job, either by suicide or from natural causes. This happens rarely, and when it does occur it affects people who likely have other severe problems and for whom the job loss comes as the last straw. When fired managers and staff talk about their feelings, the imagery they use nearly always includes reference to death and funerals. For example, one long-term manager dismissed after a corporate takeover reported:

> When they told me my job was terminated, I went through the mental and physical torment that had happened to me only once before, when my 13-year-old was killed in an accident. I can't describe the degree of trauma—the gut-wrenching thoughts, the ulcerous symptoms, the total loss of a grasp on reality—to someone who's devoted his whole life to a beneficent company that has turned into something else.

In a world where you are what you do, people who experience the abrupt loss of job and income feel suddenly worthless. It is extremely hard and embarrassing to explain one's feelings to family and friends, but it is worse to keep it all inside. At such times, their strong support and understanding are critical for maintaining a sense of self-worth, and the crucial feeling that there is still an emotional safety zone.

The connection between job loss and stress is underscored by psychologists who study what happens to people who lose their jobs unexpectedly. One of the most interesting findings comes from a "stress scale" developed at the University of Washington. There, Professors T. Holmes and R. Rahe showed that the stress produced by being fired is greater than that produced by most other life events. When enough stress events combine in a single year to score more than 200 points on this scale, psychologists predict "at least a 50-50 chance of experiencing a fairly serious breakdown in health in the following year." Firing, awarded 47 points on the scale, ranks eighth out of all the experiences we can have requiring "readjustment." It is exceeded only by the death of a spouse (100 points) or close family member (63), major illness or injury (53), and getting married (50) or divorced (73). If misfortunes strike at the same time, it is not difficult for a fired worker or manager to exceed this 200-point danger zone. For example, if you lose your job in the same twelve-month period that you also took out a new mortgage, went on a diet, experienced a drop in income, lost a parent, and found your sleep habits changing, you could become a 200-point candidate for a health breakdown.

Almost everything imaginable befell both workers and managers at a closely watched paint manufacturing plant in Detroit during the 1960s. Two years before the plant's closing, company headquarters announced plans to shut it down as soon as a new plant being built in another state was completed. The 1965 closing at Baker is the most carefully researched and best-documented account of how a large, closely knit group of workers responded to their jobs' termination and the shutdown of an operation they had thought would go on forever. Even though they had advance notice, many did not believe it would really happen and nearly everyone stayed on until the very end. Throughout this time, a pioneer University of Michigan medical team headed by Dr. Sidney Cobb kept close track of how people's health changed while the plant was closing. There is no evidence to suggest that his disturbing findings would be any different for closings in 1988. (The only detail likely to change is that the physician in the incident to follow would probably be a nonsmoker today.) In *Termination: The Closing at Baker Plant,* Alfred Slote has provided a gripping chronicle of the entire two-year closing and its aftermath. Here are some excerpts from his remarkable account:

One afternoon, Tom Morgan was sitting in his office when he heard a commotion and looked up to see a knot of men, sales people, coming down the stairs, sort of carrying, half-walking Will Calloway, who was trying to make a joke of it.

"What's going on?" Morgan asked.

"Old Will's got a little stomach upset," some said, and Will laughed.

"A ham's a ham, Tom," he said.

They made him lie down. Morgan says, "The minute I took a good look at him I knew it was no stomach upset. He was white as a sheet, but he grinned at me, and winked, and then just lay there.

"We sent over to the clinic for a doctor and we stood around Will and talked about other things. Will watched us, and pretty soon he said he felt a lot better.

"The doctor came and put a stethoscope on him, and listened to him and said what he heard sounded all right. By this time, Will was feeling real good, making jokes and telling us he wasn't holding up production now because only the supervisors were here. And he sat up and asked for a cigarette, and we all had a smoke, the doctor too, and suddenly the cigarette fell out of Will's fingers, he closed his eyes, and fell down on the bed. The doctor jumped for him, did heart massage, breathed down his mouth. We rushed him to the clinic where they had oxygen tanks, but he was gone. He'd died right in front of our eyes. A joke on his lips at the last moment."

Will Calloway would be the first of three salesmen to die during the closing of the plant. Towards the end of that year Louis Arnot would die of a heart attack at home and the following spring Harold Peterson would take his own life.

The death of Calloway depressed everyone, for he was universally liked as a good Joe.

Looking back on it, [plant manager] Frank Robertson says, "I think now how I worried about the hourly people who were going to be without jobs. Maybe I should have worried more about people like Will Calloway, Louis Arnot, Harold Peterson, Lloyd Shearer, who was so sick all the time—management people whose jobs were supposed to be the same but had to be different because the production facilities were being moved. But, you know, we met so often with the union to argue about severance pay, seniority transfer rights, pension funds—we didn't have time to worry about salaried people, about management people who had no one to represent them. They got lost in the shuffle . . . One lost his retirement pension with just a year to go" . . .

Although he himself hadn't been sick one day in Detroit [from the time he first arrived in 1925 to the final week of the plant closing in December of 1965], during that last week Robertson [the plant's manager] had attacks of pain and fever. His doctor examined him and, finding nothing, concluded it might be a virus . . . The fever did not clear up. Massive doses of antibiotics were administered. After a few days the fever went down but the stomach pain and bowel disorders lingered. Robertson went into the hospital for some tests the day after he retired in February 1966, and his illness was then diagnosed as mucous colitis—a persistently irritable colon which, according to medical literature, is mainly caused by tension associated with feelings of guilt . . .

As a salaried manager, Robertson was not [officially] part of Dr. Cobb's study—a fact Cobb regrets, for there is mounting evidence that middle and top management people are often hit harder by a plant closing than are hourly workers. Certainly Frank Robertson was a man who was hit hard, though it might be more accurate to say that Robertson hit himself hard. Robertson's phenomenal feat of keeping a plant going for two years after its closing was announced was due mainly to the fact that he cared about his people and was able to communicate his caring. It was also this

> able to communicate his caring. It was also this caring which later produced, in Dr. Cobb's words, "uncontrollable feelings of guilt, which, in turn, contribute to Robertson's colitis."

Neither Baker's management nor its hourly workers came out of this plant closing unscathed, or without showing clear signs of stress.

> Dr. Cobb's research [revealed] that out of 54 men . . . , the Baker closing and its immediate aftermath precipitated 3 cases of ulcers, 8 cases of arthritis, 5 cases of hypertension that required hospitalization, 2 cases of labile (fluctuating) blood pressure, 6 cases of depression severe enough to require medical help, 1 case of alcoholism, and 3 industrial accidents suffered by men in new jobs they disliked. In addition there were two cases of alopecia (loss of hair)—Leonard Spiess lost his hair once, and Duane Paddleford lost his twice.
>
> . . . In some cases, wives were hit harder than their husbands by the Baker closing. Cobb's nurses report that out of 54 families, three wives came down with ulcers during this period, two with arthritis. There was one case of hypertension and a case of asthma. One woman was hospitalized with mental illness during this period, one with tuberculosis, and one for skin cancer.
>
> The nurses report that four marriages seem to be in trouble since the plant closed, and there have been two divorces.
>
> In addition, children of Baker employees have been affected by the closing. Two brothers, 17 and 18, went into a mental hospital one month after the plant closed. Their father was one who came down with arthritis during this period. One 16-year-old girl, unmarried, became pregnant, one 15-year-old girl was severely beaten by her stepfather and required hospitalization. Again *the control group [of hourly employees] still working showed no such parallel upsurge in family illnesses and social problems.*

> If wives suffered along with the husbands—and in some cases more than their husbands—it is also true that many of them provided the buttressing strength that enabled their [husbands] to weather the change. Joe Nadeau, who left the plant in a drunken rage on his termination day, had a wife who worked, who supported him emotionally, who made decisions for him. Nadeau, who is extremely prone to psychosomatic illnesses and had ulcers and headaches the last three months of the closing, has made it on his new job thanks mainly to a tough and supportive wife.
>
> . . . Dr. Cobb believes that a company ought to be required by law to continue health insurance benefits for six months after a closing or until the man in question has been employed in a situation providing coverage. The Baker study shows that this is a period when expenses go up. If insurance is not available, the effects on the men can be catastrophic.
>
> . . . "The stronger men will always cope," says Dr. Cobb. "They will get out and manage whether a plant closing takes two years or ninety days. These men can see the handwriting on the wall and can do something about it. The others can't, and they get hurt . . . A plant closing is a genuine social emergency and it will be one measure of this country's greatness how well we respond to a phenomenon that will be increasingly common in the years to come."

The risk of emotional pain and dangerously high stress levels from firings increases with contentment and personal involvement with the job. The happier and more stable an employee is, the more stress will follow a separation. As an employee in an uncertain environment of business change, do yourself a favor. To reduce the aftershock of being fired, consider your alternatives at all times. Also stay alert for signs of change that can inevitably affect you and your current job. Being fired can happen to anyone, at any time, on any level at any company.

The Traumas of Downsizing

Downsizing makes it very difficult to manage people, to keep up their spirits and your own, knowing all the time that something awful is going to happen.

Executive at oil company, 1986

For managers today, fears about the future if their company is downsized, or merged and taken over, are no less terrifying than Baker's closing was to its workers and plant officials. Positions are eliminated and people lose jobs in both cases. Downsizings occur whenever organizations announce cutbacks in their size and number of employees. Downsizings now rival plant closings as a new cause of stress across corporate America. Management is far less exempt from the ax-wielding forces of "Downsize and Dismantle" than it was when the Baker plant was shut down. Today when a large plant is closed down, staff jobs in the company's front office are eliminated just as quickly as production jobs.

A downsizing differs from a unit or plant closing in that the organization does not send everyone away. In a closing, there is no question your job is gone; you know you face unemployment. The news is painful but also immediate and perfectly clear. The impact of a downsizing is different. You learn there will be cutbacks long before you find out exactly *whose* jobs are targeted. Maybe older managers will be asked to retire early. Others could be reassigned, become "stressed out," and quit. Still others will be dismissed outright.

The emotional and financial wringer of downsizing is nerve-wracking and humiliating for a company's managers. At every rank, the discovery that they are no longer in control, combined with widespread uncertainty about the future, takes its toll. When people no longer feel the system plays fair or rewards accomplishment and high performance, they are disappointed and become cynical. Often, the initial terror and disbelief turn to anger, and many workers become depressed or enraged as the atmosphere in the work setting is slowly poisoned.

In downsizings, many managers who remain feel they got to stay on only by luck or accident. Like Baker's Frank Robertson, they feel a strong kinship with the survivors of any disaster, overwhelmed by uncertainty and the guilt of "Why me?" Consider the confusion and controlled rage of marketing director Ted Wilson, promoted by an executive team of new "asset managers" after his corporation was taken over and downsized:

> You can't find it here now, but three years ago this company had a soul. It was alive. People looked forward to coming in every day. We took pride in our work. And everyone made good money. This company was no candidate for chapter 11.
>
> After we were sold and the new boys stomped in, this whole place turned into a ghost town. It really got spooky. We couldn't figure any pattern for the transfers, promotions, or firings. It's still a mystery why I am moved up, Bob gets fired, and Delores is paid big bucks to resign. They did this a lot, [making] decisions about staffing before they knew who we were. Like we were all the same, not very bright, here to take orders. Since we have no credibility, they think it doesn't matter much who gets assigned to do what. People's experience and earlier performance weren't counted. So when I got this quick promotion, we figured it was just the luck of the draw. I didn't know them and they hardly knew me, so I don't feel very grateful to anyone. I could have pulled the good riddance straw just as easily.
>
> How are things now? Well, everyone who quit or fell out the door with the division they axed had more than a few rough moments. They seem to be doing better now, but I'm not sure how things have turned out for everybody. What's amazing is how many who stayed here would be happy to burn the place down if you asked them. It's funny, but we've all just stopped caring how the company does. We used to talk about it a lot. Since the business still comes in, the new guys probably could

> care less whether we talk about it or not. They only talk to the numbers anyway, so I guess what we say wouldn't matter to them one way or the other.
>
> But I'll tell you one thing. When we drop market share, and even if the whole company collapses, a lot of us will just stand and cheer. We've been spending plenty of office time planning our way out of here, anyhow. It's not like before, when we would all warn top management if we saw trouble coming. Three years ago we'd bust our ass to keep this company on top. But no more. My future's about set. I'm glad I won't need this place for much. When these bozos make three bad calls, I'll celebrate. I hope to hell they lose their shirts.

More and more managers are joining in Ted Wilson's outrage at companies they used to love. Like Wilson, they resent the rough treatment they and their friends are being put through. They've gotten very few explanations, and doubt the wisdom and good faith of what has gone on. For many, it is like being disowned by their own family. Downsizings attack managers like an emotional buzzsaw. They shatter the belief that good job performance leads to recognition and reward by the company. Ted Wilson feels no gratitude for his promotion since he knows Bob's only reward for an equally strong contribution was a firing. He moved up but does not feel any more recognized for his value or accomplishments. He correctly suspected that the company's new executive team was gunning for high short-run performance, and then would be moving on to attack and downsize another firm.

Many of the problems managers face in any big downsizing were observed by Tyrone Hogan, a corporate staffer who quit after moving from a large acquired corporation to the new parent company's headquarters. As he vividly recalls:

> Once you've been someplace for seven years, you're rooted there, you built your identity around

> who you are there, and how you operate in that environment. You might imagine leaving there, but feel safe in assuming that if you did, it would be your own decision. Fortunately, I wasn't at the end of my career so I knew I could walk away from the funeral and still carry on. But I don't think people who are older than I am feel quite the same way. I am barely forty. But people older than me are more bitter because they look back at all those years of investing in something, in giving of something and sacrificing of themselves, in building for the future that isn't going to be there. They're very angry.

Hogan continued:

> Our downsizing ended up being the longest funeral you can imagine. Every day there was another going away party. Within six months our corporate staff dropped from almost 300 to around 35. I grew up there and thought I knew everybody pretty well. Now, all of a sudden it's like somebody turned a kaleidoscope and everybody was a little different. People change when they're scared stiff. It's awesome.
>
> It's a tough thing for people who've done real well to feel pushed out that door. It was a tough thing for the ego, like carving out a big piece of yourself. I cut a big piece out, even gave it a proper funeral. I choked up, not simply for the loss of the company, but because it was a real turning point. As much as I have an eye on the future, you look back with more than a little sadness when leaving. Whether you're in love with the company or not, it's who you were, it's part of who you are. Especially when you've been there for some time, it's like cutting out a big piece of yourself and burying it. I think the psychological reaction is very profound. It makes you question all kinds of things.

What so disturbs everyone in restructurings like Hogan experienced is that their company is reversing course, admitting defeat. Instead of growing and hiring new people, it has announced it will be getting smaller. The company is telling its own managers they should no longer expect it to provide enough work even for those already on board who thought they and the company were going to keep growing together.

In downsizings, you *don't know* if you will be told to go or asked to stay on. Everyone goes through the same fears, in anticipation of the ax. Rumors fly and people worry from week to week. Who is leaving and who will stay? Uncertainty and concern over job security last longer during a downsizing than during a department or plant shutdown. The worried survivors of downsizings are upset over the last round of cuts and fearful about the next one. When this is going on, straight answers are seldom available from superiors, who most often don't have any real idea of what's going on either.

To be caught in a downsizing is extremely unnerving. "Work environments with low information and high stress can create clinically diagnosable conditions among their members," notes Emory University psychologist Roderick Gilkey. "These include high anxiety levels and constantly looking about trying to put things together." Increased impatience and quick anger are other stress signals that can expand into hyperactive behavior resembling the Type A personality syndrome. This includes always being in an enormous hurry; for example, interrupting and finishing sentences for people who are speaking slowly. Professors Dennis Organ and W. Clay Hamner summarize additional signs from psychological studies: "The 'Type A' eats fast, walks with a snappy pace, [and] will try to read mail and sort through budget figures while carrying on a telephone conversation. . . ." Downsizing and job stress alone do not cause the personality syndrome. But unless these Type A–like behaviors run their course and get replaced by a less stress-prone profile, there is good reason to expect the subject to run a greater than average risk of contracting premature coronary artery disease.

Shock and Confusion During the Downsizing

When a downsizing is anticipated, every manager feels personally threatened by the rapid-fire barrage of bizarre edicts from the top, regardless of whether he or she is kept on or fired. The whole organization goes into shock. Shortly after a giant Fortune 500 company announced a major downsizing, Rick Morgan, one of its many middle managers, reported how he and his colleagues were getting on. Reflecting the puzzled reaction of many others in the same situation, he answered:

> It's very hard to work when you have no idea what will happen next. "Final" changes are replaced by new ones every other week. So even when you're told you survived a "final" round of cuts, you know you can still get another turn next month. No one can really know what's coming down at his level until they settle who's where on the top floors. Right now it's so chaotic you can be demoted if you stay on, but also called disloyal if you go for the exit package. Most of the people leaving looked relaxed, like now they can stop worrying about what's happening here. The ones who can't get out or want to stay anyway are the most nervous and upset.

Corporate ladders, with their once predictable rules for how to move up in the company, degenerate into random crapshoots during a downsizing. There will be no more reliable organization charts until after the dust settles. One manager in a downsized firm recently called his brother and said, "The new organization chart came down today and my name wasn't anywhere on it.

Thank God somebody only goofed and I wasn't fired." Those staying on feel less like winners than survivors, in offices that vibrate with the jagged tension you would expect to find in a war zone.

The drastic restructuring Rick Morgan describes is not unusual. Many employees fear that "life at this company will never be the same." Usually they are right. One executive in the midst of a downsizing recalls, only half-jokingly, "Whenever I left for a few minutes, I'd always tell a secretary, 'If my boss calls while I'm out, please find out his name.'"

A downsizing forces everyone to take a long, hard look at what he or she gives the corporation and can expect to get back in return. Those who remain have seen many of the company's best managers bail out for better opportunities elsewhere. They have seen friends and valued colleagues pressured to quit, bribed to take severance or early retirement, or simply axed without warning. Many sit at their desks wondering if they should have quit too.

These questions no longer involve any concern for the company's well-being. American business is forfeiting that kind of caring. Downsizings inform everyone that they are just employees passing through. While their advocates claim mass firings will produce greater efficiency in the long run, there is no doubt that America's managers feel betrayed and sold down the river.

After the Downsizing: Officewide Depression

Management consultants and Wall Street investors applaud downsizings for cutting costs, raising management quality, and increasing productivity. The basic notion of such restructurings "has a lot of appeal. Who after all, wants to stand up and be counted on the side of waste?" After posing the question, Walter Kiechel III, *Fortune*'s fine observer of corporate cultures, sends out a strong warning about downsizings' dangerous negative impacts on those remaining. Except for the "savings" gained from chopping the payroll, there is mounting evidence to challenge claims that downsized companies run better or more smoothly.

Results indicate that "companies that set out to get lean and mean too often end up depressed and lethargic instead." The claim that restructurings strengthen management blindly assumes the only ones hurt by their brutal impact are managers who should have left anyway. This hot air from Wall Street is flatly contradicted by the experience of many remaining in organizations that have been downsized.

How long does it take before managers again feel confident and comfortable with corporate life after the downsizing? One surviving manager told me his entire group is still "terrified" three years later, even though their unit is very profitable and none of them was directly affected by their company's downsizing. Another survivor, Ted Wilson, is still hurt and indignant three years later, despite his promotion. Experts agree it takes *at least* two to three years for the organization's managers to get over the initial shock, and even then, they withhold their trust. "It's one thing for a company to be created spare and efficient and remain that way, and something else for the average corporation to try to achieve this by letting people go . . . The biggest challenge . . . is helping survivors get over the multiple traumas that any large-scale cutback brings on."

One of the greatest uncertainties for managers who survive a downsizing is not knowing if it's really over. The common fear is, "I may still be pushed out in the next round." This preoccupation with becoming the next one out does not increase anyone's productivity. In fact, until the "final" cuts are made, as Andrew Sigler, chairman of Champion International, notes, "people sit around and talk . . . That's all they do. They're scared to death." Whether or not they are ultimately fired or kept on, a common reaction shared by all is "If they could do this to us, there must be something terribly wrong here."

Downsizings that cut staff to the bone almost always have a negative impact on those remaining. Laurie Jensen, an assistant treasurer at a large, West Coast–based multinational, kept a diary of what happened when the company cannibalized its own headquarters office. Nearly all survivors of the downsizing were shocked and disturbed when the initial edicts cut staff by 50 percent. Instead of being pleased at having been spared the ax, they expressed anger, grief, distrust, and a newfound fear of the company. Here are some of Jensen's entries as the atmosphere deteriorated and officewide depression set in:

> We are in a catatonic state. No one is getting involved or starting up any new programs. Many who were let go are still coming in. For eight hours a day still! I don't think they have anyplace else to go. One twenty-year guy looks real puzzled. Seems stunned and shattered. Asks how many hours is eight per day for fifty-two weeks times twenty years? He's just incredulous. It's over a month, but he still hasn't begun looking for another job yet. Another guy, hired only six weeks before his job disappeared, also comes in. He is living off his severance pay and doesn't have any reason to be here either.
>
> At the time of the initial downsizing, remember my gut feeling was they would need to dirty it up again after it's all clean and right? Otherwise everything gets too deadly boring. Now it's all come true. With people size down and jobs reallocated, what we have left is a well-oiled machine, clicking along with a lot fewer folks. And now they have nothing to say to each other!
>
> Without any mysteries left, no one feels they have an important part in a grand plan coming from anywhere. Even if it wasn't very real, people are affected in a strange way when they don't have anything like it to believe in. I sense a real reluc-

> tance by executives to clean up any more accounts because what is left is a lot of work for very marginal gains. Besides, everybody is asking, What will they do once this is done? Another round of firing? No one is doing much of anything. There really is no involvement.

Laurie Jensen had no desire to remain in this dismal work environment. She interviewed for other jobs and took one with another company three months later.

Downsizings' Negative Effects

Many observers note that downsizings at big companies often result in their losing their most talented managers, while others with far less ability and ambition are allowed to stay on. Executives who remain at downsized companies report it is much harder to challenge, keep, or promote their best people. *Fortune*'s Felix Kessler shows how this carries an ominous warning for the future:

> After all the cutbacks and retirements, top executives may find that two kinds of managers remain: those afraid to rock the boat and careerists who are not interested enough to try. Cuts made for the sake of efficiency may contain the seeds of long-term instability.

Downsizings wreak havoc on morale and productivity, both of which plunge dramatically when the announcements are abrupt, the cuts deep, and their execution instantaneous. Announcements that take everyone completely by surprise make open communication impossible at the time when it is needed the most. Such poorly planned and executed reorganizations guarantee that the resulting career jolts will be maximally stressful for both managers and workers. The stress can transform once-attractive corporate employers into unpleasant schizophrenics.

"You've got this paradox of eliminating people and, at the same time, retaining commitment among those who remain," points out University of Michigan Professor Noel Tichy.

Those who remain are plainly left to pick up the pieces. Often they have to make do, working under severe budgetary restrictions. Practically everyone who has survived a downsizing describes how feelings of "doing time" and "getting by" replaced the optimism they felt before the company dropped its bombshell. Managers put less effort into work when they lose faith in their companies; they take less pride in their jobs and stop believing official statements.

In 1985, a nationwide survey by Opinion Research Corporation in Princeton found that "employees are almost to the point of paranoia in companies that have recently been sold or made acquisitions." In addition, across all companies, "only 47 percent of the middle managers and a mere 21 percent of the hourly employees polled gave their corporate leaders a favorable rating." By 1987, corporations and top executives scored even lower in the hearts and minds of their managers and rank and file. When people feel they can no longer trust an employer, their respect for the executives in charge drops as well. Both workers and managers are more anxious about job security and their companies' futures than they used to be, and for good reason. Over one-half of the middle managers polled in a 1986 Harris–*Business Week* survey reported seeing their employer "cut back its salaried work force in the past five years." Nearly half also believed that "the wave of layoffs and buyouts of salaried staff is not about to end."

The Loss of Loyalty

> *I will give my best, I will do my best, but that does not include my personal loyalty. Loyalty is not part of service, it's an emotional commitment, and I made it once but I'll not make it again. It hurts too much.*
>
> survivor Bill Wright, after his company's downsizing

While bankers and stockbrokers fiddle like Nero, American industry is losing something precious. Completely missing from the vocabulary of financial wizards who design the profitable deals that are so traumatic for corporate managers are words like *caring* and *commitment*. Financial models exclude any consideration of a crucial "intangible" like *loyalty*. In fact, because commitment and loyalty lack a clear and simple dollar value, Wall Street does not even recognize their importance. But inside an organization, these intangibles—spirit and caring, insight and a creative spark—all go far beyond just doing one's job. They simply cannot be taken for granted.

One manager forced to think about this a great deal is Bill Wright. Wright is a junior executive who was well on his way to a good promotion before his financial institution was purchased by a "friendly" acquirer. Like Laurie Jensen, he has watched it change through the by-now-predictable downsizing that followed. Wright's disappointment and sad sense that he must now leave "home" speaks for thousands of others who have bumped up against a similar dilemma:

> This is the only company I've worked for since getting my MBA twelve years ago. We have a new team at the top, and they blame anyone who worked here earlier for anything that goes wrong. For the last year no one in this division—which always made money!—has known what we're supposed to do now. So even though my situation's not desperate, all there is for me to do is sit around all day and wait. It's almost a year now and it's driving me crazy. It has been the most unsettling experience I ever had. If I leave here and the next place is acquired, I'm going fast next time. No more waiting around for new policies like I'm doing here. It's really too bad. Somebody somewhere in the world is the loser.
>
> I know there are tremendous changes taking place in this business. Companies divesting

divisions, companies acquiring each other, entering and exiting from the market. People see themselves becoming less important in the shuffle. Big corporations look at you as another piece or pawn in the chess game rather than as a person. Well I'll be damned if I attach my life to somebody else's chess game.

Too many people, too many of my colleagues, some who are still here, those who agree with the new management and those who disagree with them, those with problems, those who don't have problems, they all agree on this one aspect—that they no longer feel loyal to the company. They will do as good a job as they can, and better, but not out of loyalty. Because someone is paying you a buck and therefore you make sure you work for it. But no more than that. That loyalty is hard to describe precisely, but whatever it is and how it is that you acquired it, in my book, it's lost.

I don't like saying this. It's not a pleasant attitude to have, but I didn't think of it myself. This has been forced on me. As a realist, as a businessman, I have no choice. It's probably going to happen in any big company, so one of the things I am thinking of is going into business for myself next. I still have a tremendous sense of loyalty to this place, even though it's already like a different organization and I will probably leave soon. I know for sure no other company will get it when I leave. No one's ever going to get that kind of loyalty from me again.

Bill Wright's refusal to invest as much loyalty and commitment in any future employers, and his despair over losing faith in the employment relationship, are echoed by managers across America. Louise Correia, an engineer with AT&T for fourteen years before it downsized, told *Fortune*'s Felix Kessler how much her attitude changed from the experience: "I failed to realize that companies really don't have loyalty to employees, just to the bottom line. Now I realize I don't owe a company my heart and soul." A recent *New York Times* feature on "The Demise of Loyalty" reported "loyal employees . . . are increasingly hard to find these days . . . Says a marketing vice president who recently started a new job after losing his previous one in a takeover: 'I'm loyal to the extent that I do the best job I can, but loyalty doesn't extend into my personal feelings anymore.'"

This quiet rebellion by managers under fire is occurring in all areas of corporate life. It has become increasingly unusual to find employees who *care* about tasks that are not required and that take time away from their personal lives. A lessened commitment to the company now enables managers to rank family and personal life higher on their new scale of priorities. More managers are refusing to relocate for their employers, and fewer expect to remain with just one or two companies throughout their careers.

No one, from the chief executive on down, cares as much for his or her company after a restructuring as before. Angry and disappointed managers feel betrayed and become much more cautious and reserved. Longtime executives resent being told to enforce deep cuts on companies they grew up in. All people affected regret having been so committed to their jobs, only to be bitterly disappointed, rejected, or simply caught off guard. Managers who have lived through a downsizing are determined to avoid intense future commitments. Most believe it is the only way to remain sane and professional within the new rules of the game.

On a broader level, there is a massive and fundamental shift under way, leading managers away from the unswerving commitments of time and energy that long have been seen as a hallmark of life in the corporation. It is that "extra mile" that managers used to run out of love for their company that is being lost. It is going out of style under the pressure of changing management practice in big corporations. Except where managers continue to believe their organizations are trustworthy, we will see extra effort being replaced by more and more people "just doing their job" and keeping their résumés in circulation. The resulting paradox, notes human resource economist Anthony Carnevale, is that "the people we expect to be the most creative and flexible now work in the most insecure environment, [which is] not a good mix. Insecurity reduces productivity since it makes people more political, [and] more afraid to take chances." To add insult to injury, the competence and integrity of managers are continually demeaned by financial analysts and raiders who seem to take special delight in telling twenty-year managers that their lifetimes of work amount to no more than useless "fat" to the corporation.

When the ax falls, no one ever admits that many fired managers are honorable soldiers downed in the savage war being waged on the future of large corporations. *Rather than publicly state excellent managers are being sacked simply because cutting their jobs makes short-run corporate profits look better, the financial press rubs salt in the wounds by screaming that restructurings rid the business world of fools and incompetents.* Raiders and financial analysts claim that employees get fired and laid off because "they deserve it." The financial world's "new" philosophy of employee relations is a brutal recipe for demoralizing managers.

In 1985, when the well-managed CBS was targeted for restructuring, this arrogant, shortsighted philosophy was invoked over and over again. Consider this typical insult from a financial analyst at the investment firm of Smith Barney, praising the downsizing of the CBS news division: "They're [just] a bunch of high-priced, underworked people suddenly having to toe the line and they can't understand it." At companies as good as CBS, which before its stock buyback had just reported record earnings in another banner year, managers continue to be embittered while investors reward their high performance by selling the firm out to the highest bidder and supporting retrenchments and mass firings.

It is these same restructurings that have created the destructive new management culture of widely shared anger, anxiety, and mistrust. These feelings are shared by winners and losers alike in the new corporate lottery for management jobs. Managers' strongest objection to the changes that accompany downsizing is that too many good people get hurt very badly and unfairly. As a result, managers' continuing personal commitment to their companies is no longer assured. It may not even be for sale. As Bill Wright put it, "no one's ever going to get that kind of loyalty from me again."

The resulting message to chief executives is that if the firm is free to sack its managers and downsize at will, it can no longer expect the same levels of commitment, involvement, and caring from its own employees. If companies downgrade what they have to offer their employees, they should expect managers to respond in kind.

The long-term effects of this loss of loyalty are dangerous for corporations. Employees care less and less about their companies. "There's absolutely no doubt that corporate loyalty is lower today than it's ever been," flatly declares an expert after examining changes in people's answers to questions about loyalty and commitment during the last twenty years. Enjoyment of work has also taken a fall. "Job satisfaction for all employees, regardless of rank, is [also] lower today than it has ever been," the *Wall Street Journal* discovered in 1985. Thomas O'Boyle found employee loyalty shattered and warned: "[This] rising disaffection has profound implications for employers . . . [as] thousands of workers have discovered that years of service mean little . . . in an era of takeovers, mergers, and layoffs."

This reaction does not change as managers advance to positions higher up on the corporate ladder. In fact, higher-level executives sound even less trusting and more disappointed. Their feelings about company loyalty suggest trouble ahead for companies hoping to find managers who will give a damn and go out of their way for the company. It is no longer reasonable to expect newly appointed executives earning more than $200,000 a year to be loyally committed to their companies.

A 1986 survey of these top managers by the executive search firm Heidrick & Struggles paints a very stark picture. This study's surprising results reveal how far our corporate system has come toward alienating its most powerful and committed leaders. The cold wind of restructurings extends into their executive suites as well as into the offices below them.

In the survey, corporate leaders reported nagging doubts about the future health and viability of big companies. They predict that many emerging corporate stars will simply walk away from the big firms they are being groomed to manage. Consider these amazing statistics. Asked if upper-level managers are "beginning an exodus from Fortune 500 firms," 73 percent of the 545 very successful executives polled by Heidrick & Struggles either agreed outright or had no quarrel with the idea. Only 37 percent had confidence in the futures of big companies. Three other surprises: Fewer than one-half were willing to relocate for their company. Only one-third believed loyalty means "support and commitment to corporate goals and strategies." Perhaps most surprising, only one-fourth would characterize an "ideal employer" as the company that promoted them into the ranks of top executives.

Big companies have cut back so deeply that by 1986, more than 300,000 unemployed managers were unable to find new positions. This is the first big oversupply of managers since World War II. It is especially devastating both to older managers and to the generation of postwar baby boomers lining up now for promotions. Before anyone climbs very far in a large corporation today, Wall Street's hit men "Downsize and Dismantle" may appear and begin chanting, "We already have too many managers. In order for you to move up, others have to move out." Then they smirk, adding: "Even then, your chances are still small. Big companies are too fat. They must slim down. The acid test of how serious they are will be how many people they fire! Then we'll find out how lean and mean they really are." This attitude pits mentors against their own protégés. In this atmosphere, loyalty is the first casualty.

Meanwhile, the financial community continues to reward the push for more firings, selloffs, and takeovers, since these increase the corporate victim's share price. Under the shadow of this constant threat, it is dangerous to put off protecting yourself from the ever-present chance of a disaster in the making. In environments where axes can fall so unexpectedly at any time, more action is required. You must look out for yourself because nobody else will. It is time to think like a free agent.

Part Two. The New Free Agent Manager

4. Free Agent Management

Corporate raiders, deregulation, and foreign competition have done a number on the noble tradition of company loyalty . . . Any remaining illusions on the subject [should be dispelled] . . . When AT&T, Eastman Kodak, DuPont, and Arco no longer provide continuity of employment, the word should finally get around that you can only count on yourself.

Robert W. Dingman
executive recruiter

If you don't have the upper hand with management, it'll rip your heart out. That's its job.

Edward F. Mrkvicka, Jr.
author of *Moving Up* and former
bank president

Theory X Creates Free Agent Managers

As we have seen, the cultural climate of large corporations has entered a new ice age. In the early part of this century the cold-blooded philosophy of Theory X, or "scientific management," dominated and dictated the treatment of employees. Many of its favorite premises are being hauled out and restored in full force today—namely, efficiency, standardization, and economies of scale. Scientific management was a no-nonsense carrot-stick style that assumed the replaceability and interchangeability of the employee. "A skill is a skill is a . . ." type of style. Since then we have come a long way. Or have we?

As industry grew and developed, so did the sophistication of the employee, and new practices were created to appease a disgruntled work force demanding more than just a wage. Theory Y arrived, nearly fifty years ago, to fulfill more of the personal and psychological needs that employees bring with them to work. To the astonishment of their bosses, employees contributed more if these needs were met on the job. The "human relations" style of management grew out of these realizations.

While implementation of Theory Y sometimes suffered from more kind words than deeds, many of its tenets carry over into more recent fashions in management. We have gone from Theory X, to Y, and now Z. During the 1980s, William Ouchi and other experts turned our attention to Japanese management practices and encouraged their imitation. Following this advice, American companies employing 50 or 50,000 have instituted Quality Circles, exercise breaks, and company slogans designed to motivate their employees and increase company loyalty.

Today many of these programs to create a corporate culture rewarding innovative ideas and productive people are ending. In their place is the harsh economic relationship reminiscent of the rough handling employees experienced during the heyday of "scientific management." Today's work force is being pushed backward in history, to that far less decent time when men and women were treated like machines, chewed up, and spit out when no longer of obvious value for the moment. Previously only workers on the low end of the ladder were subjected to such management maneuvers; they formed unions to protect their jobs. But now, neither workers nor managers are immune from the axes of Downsize and Dismantle. White-collar managers are the least prepared to have their careers so kicked around, and they are often the least protected.

Most of us were brought up to expect more from our careers, to be able to look upon our co-workers as a family, place more trust in our employers, and take comfort from meaningful activity at our home away from home. Companies creating this atmosphere are widely admired and considered to be excellently run. In a society where what one does for a living is nearly synonymous with who one is, having this source of identification suddenly taken away is a serious shock.

In fact, for almost everyone who has experienced the stress created by a merger, takeover, or restructuring, there was an initial reaction of disbelief. "I can't believe this is happening to me" was a common refrain. It is the same reaction many have reported when they learned they had a serious illness—the "this only happens to other people" response. In this time of transition, you can no longer ignore the headlines that hit the business pages on a daily basis. However, you *can* do something other than wait around for your career to become just another corporate casualty.

The lessons learned by the managers described in the previous chapter bear an important message for workers at all levels in any organization. While each manager dealt with the disruption to his or her life in his or her own way, each one progressed through the stages and recovered, but not without a cost. Many remained bitter, others became more bold, but all came out of it more self-protective and less committed to the company as they climbed back on for another cycle in their careers.

Two simple words—"Never again!"—summarize the unanimous reaction of everyone who has lived through the restructuring of a corporation. People who have found out how it feels firsthand, and want to avoid the pain of being taken again by surprise, know they must put up their own protective shields.

This is the outcome of people suffering not from burnout but from being burned. Whether they lost their own jobs or watched others lose theirs, smart workers, from the CEO down to the clerical staff, are investing less ego and self-esteem in any company or position. For their own self-protection, they have redefined their attitudes toward work.

These managers are now thinking like free agents. Like their counterparts in professional baseball, they are beginning to look out for themselves, find out how much they are worth, and consider offers from other teams. No longer willing to be pawns in a game of corporate chess, they have loosened their psychological ties to any company they may work for. Free agents make it a point always to know their alternatives, to have a clear idea of where they could jump if unexpected roadblocks arise in the present job. They work hard at their current jobs but never take them for granted. They direct much of their energy toward shaping and securing their futures.

The Free Agent Concept: Be Loyal to Yourself First

Employees everywhere are finding out today what America's star ball players realized a decade ago. Managers are discovering that they are brand-name contributors being treated like generic commodities. Until about ten years ago, these ball players were subject to a system of peonage reminiscent of the Middle Ages. Once drafted by a club, a player was required to remain with that team for his entire professional career. Its owners were free to trade or release him at will and to set salary scales knowing he could not play for any other major league team. After an arbitrator cleared the way for players to become free agents in 1976, ball players saw their salaries skyrocket, from five-digit figures to the million-dollar contracts for top players today.

The Free Agent Manager's response actually accelerates trends already afoot in American business. He or she realizes that today's employment relationship is much shorter than it used to be. If the firm needs you, then you're welcome to stay on and you may be rewarded according to your contribution. But corporate employment today, more so than just a few years ago, runs on the hard-nosed agreement by both parties that each one is contributing something that the other continues to need. And since firms increasingly view managers in this light, much more than by their years of service or demonstrated loyalty to the company, the intelligent manager has little choice but to know where else he or she would be welcome, and to deliver a similar message to his or her present company, and ask, "What's in it for me to stay on here?" Since you have less assurance than ever before that you will be kept on indefinitely, regardless of your present rank, it becomes more necessary than ever to check out your alternatives, and to push your firm to provide better incentives for you to stay with them.

While few corporate managers are locked into contracts as restrictive as baseball's formerly were, the commitment employers encourage produces an almost identical result. Managers have been mistakenly led to believe they no longer need to look out for themselves. But expectations for long-term relationships are being shattered as companies slash their work forces to be more "modern," and simultaneously scare off corporate raiders. Depending on the corporation, yesterday's anticipated rewards either are not there or may be withdrawn at any moment. When Kodak eliminated 24,000 jobs between 1983 and 1986, many saw yet another of the "last safe places to work" lose its capacity to deliver on that promise. And you know the world is changing when many other once-safe firms, such as DuPont, Motorola, and Lever Brothers, offer longtime employees strong incentives to leave earlier than they had planned. You can no longer count on a company's reputation as a decent or safe place to work, whether you've been employed there for thirty days or thirty years.

The best way to guard against unpleasant surprises is to prepare for dangerous events way ahead of time. You must accept the high probability that it can happen to you. It also means you know you can choose to leave, if it is no longer what you want, and that you also realize someday you could be forced out. As Walter Kiechel III puts it:

> Fido-like fealty is pretty much extinct . . . It took a while for management to catch the tune. Birds in the secretarial pool knew it, bees on the shop floor knew it, even monkeys in the lower branches of managerial trees—supervisors, foremen—knew it. [Only] their bosses didn't know it—that you might as well give up on being do-or-die loyal to the company. After all, goes the refrain, the company won't be loyal to you.

University of Chicago Dean Richard Thain, a wise and experienced placement counselor, adds:

> It is important for any [manager] to case his floor to make as sure as he can of where the possible future exits are . . . Looking at a job is rather like defensive driving. You worry about the fellow on either side of you and what might come careening out of the next driveway or intersection.

The most useful action a manager or worker can take right now is to imagine losing or leaving your job first thing tomorrow. Where would you go? Whom would you call? Have you told anyone outside the firm that you might be interested in joining them when the time comes? Have you a job waiting? Everyone needs a contingency plan at all times for exactly such an event. This psychological readiness is your occupational protection, the crash helmet you'll need to land safely if you decide you want to move on, or if you meet up with an unexpected accident in your current job. The psychological advantage you gain simply from knowing you can leave, if you want, cannot be overstated. It is your ticket to peace of mind in a time of uncertainty for managers at all levels. Free Agent Managers gain the advantage of knowing they are no longer dependent upon the company for either their jobs or their feelings of self-worth.

The Making of Free Agent Managers

Richard and Barbara Olsen were both employed as researchers at Atari in 1984. They watched their combined income go from more than $100,000 a year to zero when, as Barbara put it, "they came in one day and told us to turn in our badges in five minutes." The experience, in Richard's words, was "a shock":

> It was my first job out of college and I sort of expected that things would be a little more elegant in the white-collar world than just an abrupt "good-bye." I figured that my boss, whom I knew fairly well before I went to work at [Atari], would say something, but that never happened. When things get bad, knives start going into backs so fast you can't even see them. I've learned that that's always the way it is. So you have to watch—when you start hearing rumors that bad times are coming, there is no such thing as a friend, they're gone. Everyone is terribly nervous about themselves. It's only after you've saved yourself that you can start worrying about others.
>
> I had expected Atari would be around for a long time. The research we were doing was long-term by any standards, about six to ten years. So I clearly expected that I would still be around to do this work. But now I don't *expect* to be around anywhere long enough to do any substantial length of work. I'm going to be working in this industry until I die, but I no longer think in terms of what corporation I'll be at even in the next few years.
>
> I would like to be able to work for the same corporation because we all want to be able to predict our futures and change is hell. But I don't think there's anything one can do to ensure their future that completely.
>
> I'm committed to my new job in my own personal way. I understand that my employment there is based on business conditions. They have no com-

> mitment to me per se beyond their self-interests and I have no commitment to them beyond my self-interests. Which is to say, I'll be nice to them if they're nice to me.

Richard and Barbara are employed again in the computer industry and have survived subsequent layoffs at their new jobs. Both are more cautious about commitment to their current companies. Instead they speak in terms of where their skills are sought after in the *industry*. Their new attitude is shared by thousands who have learned that in large companies today, there is no built-in job security. It is no longer typical in just the computer industry and on the West Coast.

Protect Yourself

While acting as a free agent is reasonable and prudent, it may also seem like a selfish and unfulfilling strategy. If it is a difficult concept to accept, even for your own protection, consider this: no one can marry his or her company, nor vow to remain "till death do us part." As you decrease your commitment, think of the time and loyalty given to one particular company as just another stop on the journey of your own long-range career plan, a journey that can no longer always begin or end with the same company. You do not have to lose pride in the quality of your work just because you choose to jump ship or are forced to walk the plank.

Free agents know when and how to say goodbye. They know how to pack up their pride when they pack their bags. As Tyrone Hogan concluded, you have to give that period of your life a proper burial and move on. Otherwise, you waste time feeling depressed and thinking there is nowhere else to go. Take your pride and dedication with you when you leave a company. It is not only a safeguard against stress, it preserves your dignity.

In the face of the corporation's efforts to seduce its managers into a sense of commitment through mottos, company T-shirts, and team spirit, free agents keep their distance and maintain a sense of detachment. Many firms dislike this lack of personal involvement, especially among younger employees, and complain that "they only give a damn about themselves" or "they're careerists not interested in the company and jump ship for the first better offer." Such concerns about loyalty are rarely voiced, however, when companies are slashing jobs as fast as they can.

The younger work force has correctly appraised the reality of too few rungs on the new corporate ladder. They recognize there is a larger agenda going on that they, as individual employees, are excluded from and cannot control. As Richard Newman, former head of a company that changed owners three times in five years, puts it, "make the best deal you can for yourself short-term and don't worry about the long run, because the chances are you're not going to be there." Managers are meeting their companies' preference for short-term profits over long-term growth with the only appropriate and realistic response—short-term commitments.

This is not the response that many companies gear their recruitment and training programs toward, but it is the attitude millions of managers are embracing as company after company abrogates earlier promises or traditions of long-term employment. Millions of managers have learned that what counts in the long run is clearly not what they had been led to believe. Instead they have found that loyalty is no longer fashionable, nor even advised as an attitude meriting reward or advancement. "The sleepy solid citizen who stays with the company for 30 years isn't loyal, he's simply viewed as having nowhere else to go," notes Professor Rosabeth Kanter of the Harvard Business School.

Free agents know they have somewhere else to go. Having already loosened their psychological and emotional bonds to whatever company they work for, they are better able to handle the resulting chaos when the company later breaks with them.

Retaining Emotional Security

As indomitable survivors, free agents exhibit the three traits found by psychologists Salvatore Maddi and Suzanne Kobasa to best minimize stress: continued commitment to work and career; not being immobilized by change, but instead taking temporary setbacks as a challenge; and retaining a sense of control over how you will handle them, rather than letting outside events drive your every action. Since Free Agent Managers constantly work out their contingency plans and test out their alternatives in advance, they are not caught unprepared when the company unexpectedly changes course.

Being better prepared increases self-confidence and enables free agents to better cope with stressful situations. It helps them feel they are still in control so that they can hold self-doubts at bay and resist throwing in the towel. Psychologists see this as an important key to emotional and physical well-being.

Advance preparation also enables free agents to take the long view and think of job changes as more of a game than an earth-shaking event. Drs. Edward Deri and Richard Ryan of the University of Rochester have found people approaching this "inner sense of mastery" to be much happier than others who take setbacks and disappointments too personally. Comparing jobs to team sports, Dr. Ryan sees those who play for the fun and excitement of the game itself as being better off, even when they're on the losing side. If you can look at the job world as an occupational playing field where "you win some and you lose some," hit some home runs and get thrown some curve balls, the sports imagery takes on the trappings of a greater reality.

Having a "bazaar mentality" is another useful free agent orientation that succeeds. "The world is an auction block, not a Sunday school bake sale," writes the University of Chicago's Richard

Thain in his book *Think Twice Before You Take That Job.* Bargaining for what you think you deserve is another way of retaining control over important aspects of your work life. "I've worked with two generations of Americans, Canadians, and Europeans who looked at me in alarm when I suggested [this to them]," adds Thain. "What in Sam Hill do they think business is? Negotiating, trading bids, drawing concessions—these are the heart and soul of the workday in business, government, yes even in the arts."

Whether they are ball players or corporate managers, free agents' satisfaction is rooted in what psychologists call their "internal locus of control." Their motivation is not controlled by any coach or boss they wish to please. Even though they may work at a company for many years, they always retain some emotional distance from the office ties that bind and potentially blind them to better opportunities elsewhere. In this sense they act like freelancers, even if they are based inside the corridors of a particular corporation. This is not an easy way to think since we all enjoy the social rewards of the office setting and give our employers too much credit for creating them. The secret is to separate personal recognition for your *work* from the social recognition of your *worth.* Jesse Kornbluth, a freelance writer who doesn't miss the collegiality of the corporate setting, put it this way: "If you spend a lot of time around editors, they become surrogate parents. I don't look to my profession for the things my personal life should provide. I'm not looking [for] surrogate families."

While freelancers usually stay physically separate from the companies they work for, free agents are emotionally separate. Although the temptation is great, they resist becoming dependent on the surrogate family corporations create. More than anything else, it is this temptation to become part of the corporate family that managers, hurt once, say they will never be snared into again. You can always keep up with individual friends after you or they leave, but becoming vulnerable to the pain of being abandoned by the corporation claiming to be "family" is a lesson they had to learn only once.

Although very few fired managers would ever want to repeat that experience, many felt it got them back in closer touch with themselves. It was "a part of growing up professionally," says Jeanne Allen, a longtime manager whose company was taken over:

> It's like you never think about your own personal values until someone jeopardizes them, steps on them. Then, all of a sudden, you might surprise yourself at how much you back up. I wouldn't have traded it for anything in the world. As tough as it was, when I look back now, its timing in my personal life was, fortunately, just perfect. I'd been one of those people putting in fourteen- or fifteen-hour days because there was something I was getting out of it.
>
> But then I remember going out with some friends one night. I went to get dressed in my funkiest clothes and looked on the inside rack where I keep my shoes. Here were all these pairs of heels, but there were no funky shoes. There was a black pair, a brown pair, a gray pair, maybe a blue pair, but nothing at all funky. I thought—where did she go?
>
> I guess what I got out of it was that, here was a time in my life when I was starting to question what more there is for me, and who else am I besides my business card? This really just accelerated it and opened up a whole dimension which I would have gotten to sooner or later. But this just pushed it. It put my allegiances and my passions in perspective. That's really what it's all about.

When Ms. Allen had to face some serious identity questions, she rearranged her priorities and began to think like a free agent. She recalled hearing a free agent advise, "When the company gets tough, the tough go shopping," and she decided to take his advice. She shopped for and landed a good position more in line with her needs and preferences.

5. How and When to Pack Your Own Parachute

To become a Free Agent Manager, you need to build up and follow five winning career strategies. These valuable career boosters are summarized in the following maxims:

1. *Cultivate Networks, Maintain Visibility*
2. *Return Recruiters' Calls, Maintain Marketability*
3. *Avoid Overspecialization, Maintain Generality*
4. *Avoid Long-term and Group Assignments, Maintain Credibility*
5. *Keep your bags packed, Maintain Mobility*

These guidelines maximize the psychological and occupational freedom managers need to do best in a world of increasingly unreliable corporate employers. "Get Ready to Leave" was the main message of the last chapter, "Be Streetsmart and Realistic" are the bywords to master in this one. In the last chapter, I noted the pitfalls of getting too personally invested in a single job at just one company. This chapter explains the survival gear you should already be packing or know-how to get from your current employer. You will need these if you decide to leave, or get "surplussed." Learning to see the writing on the wall before the formal announcement, and being able to anticipate how new policies will fit into your own plans, are indispensable skills to have in your back pocket when times are changing.

Free Agent Strategies

Do not remain a flower that blooms unseen and wastes its fragrance on the desert air.

Richard Thain
University of Chicago
Graduate School of Business

VISIBILITY. High visibility is a key contributor to getting attractive outside offers and inside promotions. Being widely known with a good reputation for delivering the goods reduces your dependence on one company. It makes you a very desirable manager in the world of free agents and probably means you are being paid less than your current value in the marketplace.

Many fired or otherwise hurt managers find that visibility dramatically shortens the time needed to land another attractive job. While not everyone waits for such a disaster to strike, Tom Grady—the fired sales manager caught off guard by his firm's takeover in chapter 1—discovered that his visibility and outside reputation made him a "great catch" for former competitors. Grady's phone began ringing as soon as word of his unit's decimation got out. The customer base he had built turned out to be the envy of the region. Former competitors predicted that his ex-employer's market share would soon evaporate. He accepted a job with one whose marketing VP obviously appreciated his talents.

Grady fared better than most casualties of today's dismembered acquisitions and restructurings because he was visible to many outside the company. His performance was measurable over the short term, producing results that can look good and be put on a résumé. Other talented managers go through the same wrenching experiences, but then must add to them the searing emotional traumas of a much longer job search with frightful weeks of unemployment. Free Agent Managers don't wait until they need visibility to wish they had it. Work now to become more visible if your peers outside the company hardly know you are out there.

Tom Grady landed on his feet because his reputation and skill were in high demand. He now makes sure he is even more visible to managers working for other companies. In case he is ever again forced to leave on short notice, Grady has already prepared in advance by knowing where he might move and be welcome. This requires developing a wide network of contacts and an underlying "rolling stone" attitude, even though he likes his current employer; choosing assignments and promotions that maximize exposure to outsiders, or otherwise enable cultivation of like-minded managers in similar positions; and not gathering moss by focusing all of one's energies on the increasingly creaky job ladder of just one company, and on appearances only at in-house meetings.

William Fairchild, the fired oil company engineer we met in chapter 3, also benefited from following the visibility strategy. While employed there, Fairchild had developed an extensive network of contacts through outside activities such as regular participation in professional association and industry-related meetings. These came in handy when the company announced it was shutting down his facility's operation. Some of his fellow managers had a much rougher time getting comparable employment elsewhere. But these professionals were as highly skilled and as well educated as Fairchild. Many had even more experience.

But theirs was exactly the type of "experience" that makes managers invisible workers rather than free agents. Their experience was too company-specific, making them extremely valuable for only those positions that were so abruptly terminated. Unlike Fairchild, they had not planned ahead to make their skills more transferable. Their subsequent experience was more traumatic because they were less visible outside the company. Not anticipating that they might get fired and not seeking new jobs, they had less reason to maintain their outside contacts. Having to start almost from scratch to prove their value, they found themselves viewed as less serious contenders in a more crowded market. The hazards they encountered included discovering that having achieved a higher salary now made some "too expensive"; being company-specific made others "too specialized"; and having stayed at the same company too long made some "too old." These managers' lack of visibility and outside contacts only stretched out the number of months it took them to get their careers back on track.

Rather than signing up for corporate crusades that will be rewarded only by mention in your company newsletter, look at the larger industry picture. Marketable managers make sure they are visible outside the walls of their companies. They work at being known to others in their profession and industry. Establish yourself as an expert within your field and make sure others know about you. One way is to write and submit for publication an article or letter to the editor in a trade paper. The tendency of some older managers to ignore the world outside after being many years in a single company stands as a warning to their colleagues, as well as to younger workers.

To rest on our laurels is something most of us look forward to after years of dedicated service; however, it is a dangerous luxury in this period of corporate upheaval. Maintain your contacts with others in your industry through professional associations and other outside meetings. You can discover new opportunities and gain valuable ideas about how your skills could be transferred and how much they may command in the marketplace. It is always good to know your worth whether you stay or leave.

MARKETABILITY.

> *My next job is only going to last until another better opportunity comes along," says . . . a 51-year-old director of materials at a midwestern machine tools company . . . Currently, he's considering three positions, one of which would almost double his $75,000-a-year salary. But he says he will keep his résumé active after he accepts a new job. He plans to write again to the 350 search firms he has already contacted, telling them where he is, and also keep in touch with this network of friends and associates.*
>
> A Free Agent Manager, after experiencing several takeovers and restructurings, described in a 1986 *Wall Street Journal* report

Free agents know that part of the job is to be always on the lookout for a better job. They seek visibility to enhance their reputations, and work to develop talents and skills that will increase their value for other employers. In his excellent career guide, *Moving Up*, Edward F. Mrkvicka, Jr., compares job-seeking when you don't need a job to preventive maintenance for your car. If you neglect it, then "instead of needing an oil change" when something goes wrong, "you need a new engine. You waited too long to act." In terms of your career, if you interview while you are still happily employed, you can demand things you might never have dreamed of even suggesting if you had really needed the new position. And you might get them! Even when you do not, your network of acquaintances and significant contacts will have expanded and can be accessed later when you need them.

The worst time to establish your marketability is after you've been fired or when you really want out of a company. As Marilee Prescott discovered:

> It's a lot harder to get another job when you're unemployed than when you are still working. Recruiters prefer talking to people who are currently employed. It's ironic, because that makes it harder to get work when you need it most, and easiest when you may not even know when you'll be interested. To keep up with what's available in case I might need it next time around, I'll talk to recruiters anytime rather than only if I wind up out of work again. I now know that it's just good business for them and have learned they don't bite.

Not knowing about other available jobs, and not knowing where to go to find out about them are two of the most frequently mentioned regrets of fired managers. What Marilee learned is that answering calls from recruiters is in her self-interest. Some managers, even if they feel flattered, still mistakenly feel that it may be "disloyal" to their present company if they respond to a headhunter, or that it might give the impression that they are anxious to leave. These views are mistaken and needlessly self-destructive. There is no job that could not unexpectedly disappear or be improved upon. Headhunters also are quite accustomed to being politely turned down after discussing a possible job shift.

Managers should always return recruiters' calls before they are forced to. In fact, the best time to build relationships with headhunters is precisely when you have no reason to search for a new job. That only makes you more desirable. It also gives you time to become known and liked by the very people who can help you most when you may need their contacts and knowledge of the business world. Since you need to have an idea of where you can go if problems arise unexpectedly, there is no better way to start than by finding out what you are worth to others right now.

Headhunters' inquiries provide valuable information about what other positions are available and what salaries they fetch. Far from being a nuisance, they allow you to be much choosier than you could be under more dire circumstances. And being responsive to them now provides no-cost practice with interviewers; you may be very glad you did if the stakes get higher later. Knowing which experts to call on boosts free agents' careers in normal times. And if trouble does strike, it increases self-confidence and helps reduce the resulting stress.

Headhunters do not take offense if you hear them out, learn what the offer may be, and then turn it down. In fact, if they like you they will be back with another offer in the future. As executive recruiter Allan Cox, one of America's most honest and delightful headhunters, puts it:

> From a practical standpoint, the executives I admire the most are the ones that turn me down. I know it's a little paradoxical but there's no getting around the fact that when I pick up the phone and talk with someone who is courteous enough to me to say, "I appreciate the call, I'm flattered by it, I think it's nifty as hell you gave me this call, but I've got a full plate, I've been with this company X years, things are going well, I'm making a contribution and I feel the contribution is valued," I know right then and there; you know in our business we make a big deal out of the files, but that's one of the kinds of persons that goes into this file as opposed to merely the paper file or the computer file. That is somebody who . . . I want to pay attention to and *keep in mind for the future* because the next time around he or she may be a little bit more open and willing to take on a different situation, but for now I'm very impressed with that particular attitude.

Free agents take great pains to cultivate and ensure their marketability at all times. They are constantly "on the market" and have updated résumés in circulation. A Free Agent Manager always keeps open lines to headhunters, and will never say "no" to a new opportunity without checking it out first. They know, as Grace Keaton said, "if the company's commitment is only to the bottom line then your commitment better be to your bottom line."

GENERALITY. Developing generalized talents and skills is a free agent strategy that increases your marketability but it sometimes meets resistance from employers. In fact, corporations often encourage and reward specializations that tend to make managers too product- or company-specific. An exaggerated version of such "sticking to the knitting," if it catches your career, can hold you back by reducing your attraction to other employers over the long run. It makes you less visible and your skills less transferable. Professor Larry Cummings, of Northwestern University's Kellogg School of Management, notes how such occupational "typecasting" can cause career problems over the long run:

> Many older executives made the mistake of specializing [too] narrowly. They stop learning. Then, when a new technology comes along, they're lost. They also have a terrible time transferring to other fields. If you spend ten or fifteen years at an organization, you have organizational competence, a detailed knowledge of your workplace. That's valuable but it isn't transferable when you change jobs.

To avoid overspecialization, Free Agent Managers separate the generic traits of a specific job from their company's particular style. They emphasize those aspects of their work that could transfer most easily to another setting. Too often managers get caught up in the details of a particular project or campaign, and lose sight of how their skills contribute to the larger task being accomplished. Skills used in selling or production, for example, should not be thought of as confined to a single product, or even a single industry.

A critical question to ask yourself about every assignment is:

> Will seeing this experience on my résumé make me more attractive to future employers?

If the answer is "no," then you should request a different, more challenging assignment. You might also consider finding a better job elsewhere. Avoid "opportunities" that will confine you too narrowly to specializations useful only to your current employer. When offered such an assignment or "promotion," ask yourself what it will do for you in the future. If you won't learn anything that broadens your own expertise and value to others, in addition to your own company, it is unlikely that the assignment will enhance your marketability and visibility.

Free Agent Manager Herb Keane has seen two divisions wiped out in two nasty takeovers at different companies. Yet in each of three moves to new companies he has landed on his feet with a better position each time. Currently a manager of corporate financial systems at a Fortune 500 company, Keane explains how his insistence on retaining generality works to ensure his marketability:

> I keep my skills as broad as I possibly can, in Ninja form if you will. I keep myself real marketable—definitely. I will not accept a promotion or transfer in any area that will narrow me. Absolutely not, you can't pay me enough money to become an expert on our application of a new process technology 'cause I don't want to be an expert in that narrow specialization. I'd have to move out of the country to get my next job. But as manager of the corporate financial system, anywhere I go, I can say I know how to do that.

Not all specialization is a dead end, of course. Much depends on your particular job, skills, and point along a career path. Even if you are a valued and specialized researcher or engineer, ask yourself if the skills you are developing in your job are valuable only to your company. Specialized skills work most to your advantage if they are in areas that are in wide demand and in areas not too narrowly defined. After an unexpected restructuring, a former manufacturing company executive was able to move quickly to another company developing innovative technologies. His explanation for why he was picked up so easily is simply, "I always keep my engineering skills very broad." His broad skills were valuable after the restructuring, when he saw many executives cashiered but unable to recover as quickly. Those who encountered the most difficulty finding new employment were the executives who were most product-specific in their orientation.

If you are working in a new industry and possess a skill currently in demand and hard to locate, overspecialization may work to your advantage. However, you should be forewarned that as your specialized skill becomes more widely learned and understood, your value as a specialist may decrease and your future career opportunities become more limited.

Free Agent Managers seek to avoid being typecast as overspecialized. Develop and maintain transferable skills that will enhance your value to other employers as well as to your present employer.

CREDIBILITY. Free Agent Managers are always prepared to state their achievements clearly and articulate the valuable activities they personally perform, contribute, or supervise. They know if they cannot show what they have done, they will lose the credibility needed to stay marketable. Not having hard numbers or a clear job description is a problem for a manager who needs to document his or her claim to high performance and a strong track record.

For this reason, Free Agent Managers should avoid long-term assignments and resist being made part of a group where individual contributions and performance are hard to measure. Consider how each of these job descriptions weakens your résumé:

> I developed an ambitious three-year program to __________, but company cutbacks in the second year made it difficult to assess. Unfortunately, I can't provide hard information for my last three years.

Or:

> I was part of a six-person team which altogether accounted for a $400,000 increase in sales during 1986.

The risk of long-term assignments and being part of a team is that it makes a manager less credible as an individual. Both increase your vulnerability in today's short-term world, and make you more dependent on your employer by making it harder to show anyone outside the firm how your work contributes to the bottom line. Company-specific jobs put you at the mercy of unwritten promises from the company—to stand by a new project until its completion; group work postpones your reward for joining an "all for one and one for all" team where individual assessment is difficult. When the company breaks its promise, or you need to document your individual contribution to the team, you have nothing to show. As companies become increasingly unreliable, putting too many eggs in just one company's basket exposes naive managers to increasingly dangerous risks of future unemployment.

Free Agent Managers know that even though teamwork is touted as the key to making employees productive and companies excellent, it threatens credibility by diluting and obscuring individual contributions. Unlike free agentry, teamwork emphasizes the supremacy of group efforts over each individual's value and visibility. While being part of a team may be a satisfying experience, it also downgrades your marketability.

If you possess more unique skills, better talents, or deeper insights than other team members, be especially wary of letting your occupational identity become merely "part of that group."

Instead, identify situations that let you shine, stand above the crowd, and gain the recognition you deserve. One of the best reasons given by Free Agent Managers for taking a job with another company is that they couldn't turn down the jump in visibility that came with the new position. The lesson is to accept only promotions or transfers that enable you to increase your individual credibility.

Gaining the reputation of a "most valuable player" is a proven career builder. It makes you more visible and increases your chances when requesting assignments that will enhance your generality as well. Within companies, individual credibility also raises the odds of being asked to remain with the company if it gets involved in a merger or acquisition. Following this free agent guideline should help you avoid the sad situation of needing to account for your years in a job, without being able to marshal a credible evidence of what you alone did and succeeded in accomplishing while there.

MOBILITY. Free Agent Managers keep their bags packed and are always open to the idea of moving. This guideline cuts across and drives all of the other free agent guidelines. It is the all-purpose strategy, good for adventure or self-defense. The mobility guideline is of major importance for insisting managers prepare themselves for opportunities and surprises that can burst in on them at any moment. What's new here is not that modern managers are mobile, but that the time span between changes is briefer and less orderly. As cowboy financiers continue to force restructurings, Free Agent Managers are wise to think of themselves as more like mobile gunslingers ("Have Skills, Will Travel") than loyal ranchers underrecognized and waiting to be overrun.

If you are a manager today, you are less likely to spend your career at a single company than ever before. Free agents who pack their own parachutes gain more control over the threat of enforced mobility we are all facing, whether we prepare for it or not. Frequent job-hopping is already the norm in some industries, while others are forcing their managers out into the market by downsizing. Building your marketability, credibility, visibility, and generality ensures more choices in this more mobile corporate world.

If you are undecided about following free agent guidelines to increase self-protection, consider the dilemmas faced by managers forced into finding other positions after following the opposite course. Their *un*marketability, *in*visibility, *over*specialization, and *non*generality can only work against them. These entail an immobility, which is reinforced by focusing too narrowly on your company over your field or industry, and on your present job rather than your life career plan.

Probably the most aggressive advocate of keeping your bags packed is *Moving Up*'s author Edward F. Mrkvicka, Jr. He counsels changing jobs at least once every three years, and running blind ("Position Wanted") ads in your field's trade papers while employed, to see what other jobs are available in your area.

However far you choose to go in this direction, you should work to develop your most marketable skills and accumulate a strong track record. These are most helpful in lining up alternatives so you can comfortably move on when you need to, or decide it is time for a change.

To Leave or Not to Leave.

As mergers, downsizings, and restructurings roll on, you will face situations requiring a constant awareness of your own goals, and a reassessment of whether your company can meet them. Your job and security are at stake, and the need to decide between staying on and seeking better opportunities elsewhere will affect every manager. For many, the hardest part about making the decision to stay or leave is that we find it unsettling, and we neglect thinking seriously enough about our own careers. Most people remain unprepared until they encounter a serious problem.

Following free agent strategies establishes the psychological distance you need to feel less personally involved in your present job and imagine working somewhere else instead. These strategies force you to assess yourself objectively and plan to profit from your strengths. As thinking about your career becomes more routine, making the tough decisions should come faster and easier. The guidelines of free agent thinking position you for the best and worst in the world of today's job settings.

If you are in one of the best settings, there is no reason to think a free agent strategy would dictate that you should leave. It insists, however, that you know where you could land if your "perfect job" were to disappear or turn into a nightmare tomorrow. Acting like a free agent now enables you to stay longer at companies in trouble, when you want to, precisely because you know ahead of time where you can land if the other shoe were to drop.

KNOWING WHEN TO LEAVE. Bill Wright survived his company's "friendly" takeover, and watched as most managers in his division either jumped for the exit package or responded later to the new management's clear desire that they leave. Wright was pleased he had not been fired, but confused about what his job was now and still waiting for a clearer job description. Asked why he didn't just pick up and go, Bill answered simply, "What would you rather do? Stay in your office and rot, or take six months' salary and rot?" While he was unhappy, bored, and sitting around with nothing to do, he was more frightened by the thought of leaving.

Taking pride in not having been fired, while reporting to an empty office with nothing to do day after day, is a classic case of denial. Yet this is an all-too-common reaction by understandably scared managers—hoping "maybe things will get better, since I haven't been fired." Bill Wright was hanging on in a situation he called a "Mexican standoff" with his company. He was in a state of limbo. From the standpoint of free agent management, waiting and waiting for a positive sign long after the storm of a takeover or reorganization has subsided is akin to a slow form of suicide.

Too many managers fall victim to this trap. Not choosing is dangerous because it avoids taking responsibility for your own future and only puts off making tough but necessary decisions. "Choosing not to choose" is also unhealthy because it encourages defeatist thinking—believing everything is beyond our control, and that we bear no responsibility for how things turn out. While his passive stance seems curious to outside observers, Bill Wright's reaction is not unusual. It is a symptom of survivor shock exhibited by those who are spared, after they watched their unit cut down and their friends flee or get pushed out. When miraculously they're still there, they don't know why they were chosen to remain. Many feel guilty about their "good fortune" but just continue reporting to what may now be a rotten job.

What makes managers like Wright afraid to take the plunge and leave is that, psychologically, they spend an enormous amount of energy on everything but *letting go.* Besides the security of being in the same place that had been his first and only job since graduation, Wright had another fear he was avoiding—the fear of being fired. This paralyzed him, even though when asked how co-workers who left or were forced to leave had fared, he knew "most of them have done well. Ours [is] a highly specialized division and if you're skilled, finding a job is not a problem."

But Wright was also afraid of "the stigma if you're fired. He feared that

> out in the market it's difficult to explain these things. If you were interviewing me for a job, I don't know how many of these things you would buy as true reflections of the new management and how many you would see as my fault. You might think, "You screwed up so *you* got fired."

> It will be difficult to convince the prospective employer I didn't do anything wrong, that it's the circumstances. Even if you're very good at what you do and find a job, you may not find the job you deserve. You may have to accept a much lower one than you would get otherwise.

Wright's fear is a popular misconception. To simply assume being fired by a new management always makes you look bad to other employers is a misconception well worth disproving. Wright should have been out looking for other positions, especially while he was still employed. By not looking even when he knows he may be forced out any day, he is missing his opportunity to act like a free agent and check out the market *before* circumstances leave no other choice. Managers following Bill's example lose out on learning their alternatives by refusing to go out and test the water.

Because so many companies have forced excellent managers out in the past few years, the stigma of being fired has diminished dramatically. Displaced managers, from Lee Iacocca (before going to Chrysler) on down, are in very good company. Many have taken the mobility plunge and done enormously well. Free Agent Managers are not stigmatized by being self-protective and looking around. Unfortunately, by ignoring this guideline, Wright cut himself off from alternative avenues and the renewed self-confidence and self-esteem a better job can bring.

If Wright were a Free Agent Manager, he would have had a career plan that did not end with his now-lost dream of staying on with a promotion in the same company. He has transferable skills and credibility from his old job, but is still doing nothing to achieve the visibility, marketability, and mobility he now needs. Failing to follow these guidelines will mean having less to bring to the table and show recruiters when the time comes. Since Bill wants to remain in the same industry, we can easily outline the career plan he should have constructed for himself.

Preferred industry—Financial Services
Type of position and salary sought—Regional Account Manager at $45–60,000
Type of company I like best—Medium to large, growing. More enjoyable colleagues than I have now.
Positions desired within 3–5 years—Vice President, National Accounts
Goal 8–10 years from now—Senior Vice President
Preferred location—Midwest or East Coast city with easy access to financial markets.

Think about your answers for the same categories, and compare them to what you have right now. How closely do the field and industry you are in and the salary you are making now match up with how well you feel you should be doing? Are you achieving your goals by staying with the same company? And if not, how closely do the alternative positions you think you could find match what you are seeking? These preliminary answers should get you thinking about how committed you are, and should be, to your present job. More free agent thinking is especially desirable if, like Bill Wright, you are just going in and "doing time."

RESTRUCTURINGS ARE MORE DANGEROUS THAN REORGANIZATIONS. If you see changes under way at your company, when should you shift gears from following free agent guidelines at your own pace to a full-fledged red alert? If the reorganization is responding to "normal" ups and downs in the company's sales and profits, it is usually operations-related and should not threaten many managers directly. Outright firings and forced early retirements are still unusual.

The operational reorganization is generally designed for the long term and is likely to build in a spot for most managers already on board. You still know the players, can piece together what is happening, and can pretty well calculate how it will affect you. If you do not come out on top, or find your career blocked or dead-ending, you can circulate your résumé, act like a free agent, and still negotiate hard with other employers for the best deal possible while staying right where you are.

Everything changes, however, as soon as you hear rumors of a coming merger, a takeover, or a big stock buyback involving your company. Then it is time to rush to the phone, activate your networks, and announce your potential availability for good jobs and emergency landings. After taking these precautions and lining up potential alternatives, *then* you can afford to sit back more comfortably and wait to see what develops closer to home.

As we have already seen, these drastic corporate changes are finance-driven. They go far beyond operations and usually mean there will be a greater emphasis on short-term results, fewer jobs overall, and less opportunity. In the wholesale restructuring, more axes fall on more managers than in the case of operations-driven reorganizations. When Bill Wright's company was taken over, for example, his downfall had nothing to do with his performance, which had been excellent. The new executives, new policies, and new debt, all of which came in with the restructuring, simply had no use for his department or future services. He should have responded much more quickly by finding and checking out positions at other companies and taking the best one available.

If your firm is restructured, where will you fit into the new picture? While everyone hopes his or her job won't be disrupted or disappear when this happens, some unpleasant surprises usually are sure to follow. As we have seen, the right questions to always keep in mind are "How *much* will I be affected?" and "How different is the corporation I now work for?" Regardless of efforts by companies to reassure their managers, there is absolutely no reason to believe serious changes won't follow any corporate restructuring, or that you aren't working for what effectively is now a different company. This is especially true of mergers and acquisitions, for here even the same top executives promising "no changes" may not be around long or retain the power to deliver on their promises.

In the midst of these uncertainties, it is critical to stay alert and levelheaded as you try to estimate the extent of the damage. If your company starts to feel like a M*A*S*H unit, are the new people deciding your fate now more like Hawkeye's benign Colonel Sherman Potter, or like the tank named after the more ruthless General Sherman of Civil War fame? Hardheaded answers to questions like this will be enormously important in helping you arrive at the decision to stay or leave, while it remains your choice.

Free Agent Managers think about leaving faster when finance-driven changes loom on the horizon, because these are less likely to allow for merit-based decisions. Instead, you are more likely to see blanket early retirements encouraged and special exit windows opened for large numbers of employees. If too few managers agree to quit for the money offered, then outright firings begin. All this is far more stressful and threatening than most operational reorganizations, which create some winners and far fewer victims.

Managers are caught totally unprepared by most restructurings, because these come on so quickly that there is precious little time to get ready if you haven't already thought about what you would do. Many first find out about these drastic changes (with more to come) on the day they are officially announced. Some rushed and poorly planned billion-dollar restructurings are crafted in less than two weeks by panic-driven top managements.

For many who knew it before a restructuring, their company may seem unrecognizable. Tensions run high and the uncertainty and lack of communication make it difficult to obtain reliable information. A few find they are truly needed and move up in the new organization. Many try to lie low, hoping they are too far removed from the front office to be seriously affected by any changes at the top. While the majority of employees hope to be retained as long as their divisions remain, it can be self-defeating retained as long as their divisions remain, it can be self-defeating to remain hopeful and hang on too long when there are no positive signals from higher up. Guard against making Bill Wright's mistake of postponing the inevitable and losing valuable time.

If you get caught in a restructuring, look at your career plan and consider how your goals are aided or held back by these changes. Try to determine whether your area will be cut back, or how the overall changes will affect your prospects for climbing up the in-house career ladder. You must also weigh if and how much these "atmospheric" changes alter your willingness and desire to remain.

Free agents (and free spirits also) take these questions seriously. If you feel emotionally or economically threatened by changes in your company, you should be testing the water outside by making inquiries and following free agent guidelines. You might discover that your situation looks better than you realized, or you may find more attractive opportunities elsewhere. But you'll never know, either way, if you sit in your office and never try to find out.

Assessing Your Risks in Acquisitions and Restructurings

If your present company is merged or acquired, you must assess your new prospects for continued career advancement. To avoid unpleasant surprises, you need to know the right questions to ask and do some research on your current and future employers. You will have a much better idea of whether to bail out or stay where you are if you know about

- the acquiring company's motives for purchasing yours, and expectations for what is to come from it;
- its history and reputation for treating acquired managers with dignity, or with cattle prods;

- the financial health of your own firm and its new or likely acquirer; and
- the stock market's assessment of your company if it has not been taken over or restructured. Is it on any "buy" lists for investors as an attractive merger or takeover target?

MOTIVES AND EXPECTATIONS. The acquirer's motives can range from stripping your company's assets and selling off your division to wanting to get into your business and rewarding you handsomely for staying on board. In the first instance, you should of course be ready to leave before being told to go. But in the second, it may be possible that the company's new owners really intend to deliver on all their great-sounding promises.

After Fairchild Camera was acquired by Schlumberger, a serious conflict of cultures soon emerged, and there was no question about which set of managers would call the shots. Schlumberger's staff was in charge and was not threatened by the clash of management styles. But if you were one of the Fairchild managers reportedly told by a Schlumberger executive, "You are frogs we will teach to be princes," it should not have taken you long to put every free agent strategy you know into motion.

Signals like those that Cooper Industries sent managers at acquired electrical equipment maker Crouse-Hinds should also be seen for the threats they are and not be ignored. Soon after the purchase, managers at Crouse-Hinds's headquarters saw Cooper march in and dismantle its boardroom, taking its best furniture and coffee service to outfit its own headquarters in Houston. When an acquirer so quickly demonstrates a lack of respect for symbols of your company's past glory, you should take notice and be on guard. *Fortune*'s Myron Magnet reports that this "seemingly trivial instance, the pillaging of [their] boardroom," later became "a symbol of the takeover's whole spirit. Things meaningful to them were swept away by an acquirer who cared nothing for them or their achievements." As productivity fell, good managers sent out résumés and welcomed all calls from headhunters. Magnet's critical assessment of what followed is instructive:

> Cooper didn't just reduce Crouse-Hinds administrative staff, something that happens in most mergers and yields some of the savings such deals are designed to produce. It went further, forcing out or demoting key operating managers and striking fear into employees down the line . . . Cooper staffers overran Crouse-Hinds headquarters with high-pressure, conflicting suggestions about how things should be done . . . Cooper's treatment of a successful outfit like Crouse-Hinds is a textbook case of what management consultants say can lead to erosion of morale and productivity, and ultimately to disappointment with the deal itself.

While different situations leave room for ambiguity and may require more time to sort out, managers should insist on seeing concrete actions taken by the acquiring firm, from the top down, before believing they are truly welcome and can again look forward to a strong future there. After Allied Corporation acquired Bendix, Allied's top executives quickly flew to meetings with over 10,000 employees worldwide, to answer questions and explain how they would have a green light for continued advancement under the company's new ownership. This was a positive signal. Allied then demonstrated concretely how much they wanted the Bendix management to remain.

Representatives from both companies were given equal authority to devise and implement the merging of computer operations and staff functions rather than the wholesale replacement of one group by the other company's people. Any terminations due to the merger were worked out carefully and early, so that where bad news was delivered, it came swiftly. This minimized the time many managers had to spend wondering and worrying if they would still have an assignment after a merger. Out of a Bendix work force of 70,000 employees, only one unit (formerly Warner-Swasy) was adversely affected. Otherwise, fewer than 300 were "surplussed."

Another signal to those remaining was the care taken by Allied to see that the departing managers left well-outfitted with survival gear. For those asked to leave, Allied provided a professional outplacement service, continued benefits, sweetened early retirement arrangements, and as personalized a severance package as the law allows. Most Bendix managers have stayed on and prospered. The acquirer's motives and expectations were clear from the beginning, and the positive signals Bendix's managers received were concrete and positive.

While the Allied-Bendix merger is what most acquired managers should hope for, it is rare for a takeover or restructuring to unfold with so few casualties. Fortunately, the question of how to predict risks run by those most affected has long been a subject of study by management experts. One of the earliest and still best vulnerability checklists for acquired managers comes from a classic article by John L. Handy in the *Harvard Business Review*:

1. Did the new owner buy your company for management talent, including yours?
2. Are you the key [manager] in a profit center of vital interest to the new management?
3. Are you flexible enough to report to a new group of executives, function in a new organization structure (i.e., decentralized), and do things "their" way?
4. Are your executive skills transferable within the new structure?
5. Was your company acquired for nonmanagement reasons (e.g., special financial advantages, manufacturing facilities, or its distribution setup) of which you are a part?

6. Is your salary high in relation to the compensation scale of the purchasing company?
7. Is the salary for your job high relative to the "market" for similar positions?
8. Is your function duplicated in the parent company?
9. Were you publicly against the merger?
10. Are you in a staff position?
11. Are you a "self-made" man with long tenure?

Negative responses to the first five questions and positive ones to the remaining six each increase your vulnerability to firing or career blockage in a new merger or acquisition. The higher your number of these "wrong" answers, the more quickly you should line up and consider alternatives to your current job. Management by distant memo and an increasing sense of isolation from decision-making centers often result if you do not. Porter Farrell II, a former financial executive at a company acquired by Tenneco, considered this and left when "it was clear to us they were buying assets rather than management. We hardly ever saw them and I didn't meet with anyone from Tenneco so it was a good bet they didn't need me."

REPUTATION AND TAKEOVER HISTORY. Knowing the history of a firm your company is merging with or being acquired by can give you valuable insight into what will become of your job. The company's reputation from previous takeovers also provides clues about its likely motives. Imagine you have friends at a stable, centralized, seniority-respecting company just acquired by a hard-charging, bottom-line corporation such as GE. If you know they don't want to change much, you already have two good reasons to suggest they make sure their parachutes are packed for a better landing when it's time to bail out.

If the acquiring firm is a large company, getting information about it should not be difficult. Look up its coverage in newspapers, business magazines, and the trade press. The business press is flooded with articles on corporate performance and company styles, industry outlooks, takeover artists, and other valuable information. Major periodicals provide libraries with annual in dexes telling what news stories they have run, with listings by company.

Also consult books that rate companies' work environments, like *The 100 Best Companies to Work For in America.* Ask people what they know or have heard about the acquiring company. If you have a business degree, ask your school's staff and check its alumni directories to find managers you may know who are working there.

Although none of these sources will be totally accurate, the combined information will provide a useful feel for what you may be heading into and help you decide if you want it. Asking around should also give you a greater sense of control than relying exclusively on official channels, which usually take longer and give even less reliable information.

Finding out a positive merger history, such as Allied's, or a string of negatives about the acquirer, arms you with useful information. When TWA's pilots and other employees heard that the company's board was about to endorse a takeover bid by Continental Airlines' chief Frank Lorenzo, they marched straight to competing bidder Carl Icahn and negotiated paycuts of nearly 25 percent in return for his taking over the airline. TWA employees begged Icahn to take over the company because they knew that when Lorenzo took over Continental, he provoked one of the longest and most bitter walkouts in airline history by filing a bankruptcy claim, which voided all existing contracts. Knowing the history and reputations of both potential acquirers enabled TWA's work force to exercise more control over a bad situation. They selected Icahn as the lesser of two evils, and succeeded in making him winner of the fight for their company.

While few takeover outcomes are decided this way, the lesson TWA supports is that it pays to learn about those you will be dealing with early on and before it's too late to protect yourself.

> MANAGERS' VULNERABILITY TO EMPLOYER'S DEBT AND STOCK PRICE.
> *Hobson Brown, Jr., managing director of Russell Reynolds Associates, recalls an executive his firm recruited for a software company. "He wanted to know what will keep this company independent, how is its new product developed, does it have enough capital?" says Mr. Brown. "It's changed from, 'How do I get on this rocket going to the moon?' to a more analytical approach. There's no question people are doing their homework more."*
>
> *Wall Street Journal*, April 25, 1986

In the period from November 1986 to April 1987, such large and "safe" employers as Gillette, Goodyear, Hilton International, Burroughs-Sperry (now Unisys), Holiday Inn, AT&T, United Airlines, Safeway, and Lucky Stores announced steep employee cutbacks due to restructurings. Each one caught managers off guard who had not taken free agent precautions and planned for this stressful disruption. Knowing the financial condition of a company you depend on, and investors' beliefs about it, is of critical importance for minimizing your risk of being left hurt, hanging, and caught by surprise.

If you work for a corporation that has not been restructured, you need to estimate how exposed it, and you, are to the danger of being hit by one in the near future. You need to gauge when your present company, or any company you may be thinking of joining, will be turned inside out by this nerve-jangling event.

A good place to begin is by looking at it from the singleminded and coldhearted standpoint of well-financed, professional stock speculators. (This assumes that shares of the firm are bought and sold on a stock exchange.) Speculators' hit-and-run actions are most likely when the firm's stock is selling for less than its "book value"—the price investors would get for each share if the firm were liquidated. Ask any stockbroker to tell you if your company is in a vulnerable situation, and if so, how large the gap, or "spread," is between its current stock price and book value per share. Computing this number is a routine part of detecting restructuring tremors, which has become a highly respected and very profitable game for investors and their advisers. The farther its share price lags below book value, the more likely its stock is to be bought up by speculators interested in forcing the company's sale or restructuring.

Whether or not the firm's share price remains above its book value, a second indicator that it may become an acquisition target is the present exchange rate of the U.S. dollar relative to foreign currencies. As the dollar's value fell in 1987, the cost of buying U.S. companies dropped for Japanese and European acquirers.

You have easy access to a great deal of other useful information about the image and finances of any big company with shares traded on Wall Street. Its proxy statements and the "10K" report it files annually with the Securities and Exchange Commission often provide information that may surprise you. For instance, you can learn which other companies or individuals own big blocks of shares in it. This information may be obtained from the company, of course, but it is also on file and available at the SEC's branch offices in major cities. For those especially curious, a more detailed computer readout of who actually owns the company can be purchased from research services such as Disclosure, Inc., in Washington, D.C.

Good libraries, investment guides such as Moody's or *Value Line*, and the business press are also information goldmines. You can find many corporate disasters-in-the-making being casually discussed and predicted in business reports and financial columns, well in advance of their occurrence. Is your company on any published lists of likely candidates for merger, restructuring, or takeover? Managers at corporations written up as "on the block" or "in play" should go on red alert. If a firm is rated near the bottom in *Fortune*'s surveys of corporate reputations (published every January), it is a likely bet that a takeover or restructuring is not far down the road if not already in the works. Like investors and stockbrokers, you should always have your antennae tuned in to these sources of outside information.

Other important financial information you should know about concerns the company's amount of long-term debt. In 1986, fully 50 percent of all pretax corporate profits went to pay off these loans. You should know what percent of assets and future earnings any company that is important to you has already committed to its creditors. You can get this information from the company's annual report. Look at its balance sheets to find how much of its "Costs and Expenses" were for "Interest Payments" or "Expense on Indebtedness." These payments contribute to the gap between "gross" and "net" income. They must be made before salary raises and new ventures can go forward. If they eat away too large a chunk of what otherwise would be included as net profit, they slow down company growth and the speed at which managers can climb its career ladder.

Most firms with a long-term debt totaling more than 50 percent of their assets have already gone through a Wall Street–imposed restructuring. This means they have also experienced one or more recent waves of early retirements and wholesale firings (or "voluntary" work force reductions) like Goodyear's and Arco's. Unlike companies that have so far avoided such oppressive debt levels, a highly leveraged company is "safer" from another restructuring because there is less money remaining to be borrowed or squeezed out by large investors. If you are being recruited by or have remained with an already-restructured company, an ironic benefit is that your job may be safer there than at a more vulnerable company that hasn't yet gone through the same wrenching experience. But at the same time, you should check out how able they will be to "grow" your area at a time when so much of their earnings and cash flow is committed to bankers and bondholders.

DON'T JUMP TOO FAST. A very important rule followed by Free Agent Managers is *Never leave on an impulse without knowing where you are going next.* In the heat of a merger, takeover, or restructuring, when anxiety levels and rumors of impending disasters rise to fever pitch, you may be tempted just to walk out the door and free yourself from all the surrounding craziness. While you may get angry at your present situation and impulsively decide "anything would be better than this!", rushing off hastily can be every bit as dangerous as hanging onto a bad job too long. For all but the independently wealthy, walking out in disgust is an expensive and needlessly risky proposition. Don't quit or announce you are leaving until you have your next job in hand. Although the impulse may be right, that's all it is—an unconsidered, hasty moment of passion.

When critical decisions about jobs and careers must be made, calm, cool judgment backed by reliable information is what you need. In fact, at these times, passion alone cannot be relied on or trusted. Let's say it is six weeks after the fatal announcement that your company is about to go through some major changes in response to financial demands from Wall Street's finest. A few objective facts about life after restructurings should help cool down even the hottest emotional reaction.

Companies prefer to exhaust voluntary means of separating managers from their jobs before resorting to firings. As we shall see, that is one way for companies to avoid lawsuits they can all too easily lose. If you leave "voluntarily," you have done your company a big favor. Since this severing of ties is almost never performance based, you lose twice if you give such a big favor away without first assuring your own future. Rather than slinking quietly out the door, smart managers are demanding as much as they are entitled to get from their companies. These firms know they owe you for all the years they encouraged you to expect better treatment than you are getting now. But the companies aren't saying they know, and they hope you will forget and walk away quietly.

Quitting on an impulse deprives you of continued salary and benefits, an office address, phone, and other perks you should hold onto, even as you are looking for a new position. Without having another job already lined up before leaving, you not only lose these benefits, but also begin to drain whatever savings you had to fall back on. Recruiters will be impressed that you quit before coming to them, but not in the positive way you might have expected. As we have already heard from managers who went through this experience, it hurts your chances for the new job if you have to announce you are presently unemployed or "between positions." This must be faced up to, and can be handled if you were fired, but to voluntarily quit before packing your parachute only penalizes you for your impulsive action.

This is one of the reasons Free Agent Managers keep their eyes open to new opportunities at all times. They do not have to play catch-up under pressure to find out how marketable they are if the time to leave comes up unexpectedly. This also enables free agents to avoid making serious career decisions based on momentary passions, such as anger, panic, and fear, in the face of stressful and unanticipated changes in their companies. Thinking ahead and having contingency plans ready when times get rough are the precautions that enable them to better predict, understand, and control the situation around them.

A second reason to avoid jumping too fast is that when you react out of panic, you may wind up needlessly rushing headlong into a worse situation. Most managers do not get fired immediately following a merger, takeover, or restructuring, and the actual number fired remains a small percentage of those employed by the company. The majority of those already on board will be kept.

While the majority will not lose their jobs at the company, what is most nervewracking in restructurings is that no one can predict if he or she will be among those who are fired. But even those who will be let go usually have time to look outside while they are still on the payroll, that is, if they don't procrastinate. The majority of managers have time to do this while still at the company. Whenever this opportunity is open to you, it is the best course to follow.

While still on the payroll, you also have more time to observe how the restructuring is turning out. Staying on while testing the outside waters buys valuable time in both settings. When the choice is still yours, take full advantage of it. Following this free agent guideline is your best insurance for landing on your feet, either way. It makes your company only one of the possible candidates for your future employment and allows you to judge its new working conditions and long-range prospects on an equal basis with the other firms you are considering. Learning what each has to offer enables you to keep your options open while deciding which one is best for you. Some managers, like Bill Wright, may decide to "cash it in" and stay in a downgraded position at the same company, no matter what.

While Free Agent Managers would not follow Wright's example, they would consider staying in their present positions, even after a restructuring, if they discover it still offers better opportunities than comparable positions at other firms. To entice you to move, the new position should offer more than the same job you are doing right now. Such lateral moves seldom make you more marketable, but still impose the costs of getting acquainted and having to learn "how things get done" in a whole new setting.

The decision to stay or leave should come only after you have coolly and dispassionately assessed the pros and cons of each option for you, professionally and personally. Efforts to compare your present and a future position on dimensions of job security, prospects for advancement, opportunities to develop personally, and each company's vulnerability to new dictates from Wall Street should precede the final decision. Since your restructured company may be the beneficiary of this important free agent career exercise, it is all the more appropriate to remain on its payroll while conducting it.

If You Are Fired

The day of "come work for us forever" is long gone. A lot of folks are getting wasted in restructurings.

Rudolph Dew, Hay Career Associates

Massive layoffs have come upon us heavily in the last five years. Now, we're laying off the "good guys."

Frank Dickson
Chase Management Associates

No matter how tough you think you are, being forced to change jobs is a stressful and crushing blow to the ego. Even though we all know it's happening to *other* people every day, the emotional impact of being told your job is gone is enormous. No matter how distanced or "objective" you try to be, no one gets off undamaged. have seen how the stress of being fired can cause symptoms ranging from a greater vulnerability to colds to psychological depression. Managers holding attractive positions experience a great loss when these jobs are taken from them. Losing a valued job typically puts people through the same stages of grieving associated with the death of a loved one: initial disbelief, followed by anger, then bargaining, grief, and finally, acceptance of the fact. Being fired is an extremely difficult experience for anyone. Don't hold it in and don't pretend; letting others know what has happened to you is extremely important. Business associates who would help you land on your feet cannot go into action for you if they don't know about your changed circumstance. You should also confide in family, friends, and acquaintances so they can provide the social support you will need, and better understand your moods and behavior as you start to react.

After the initial shock, the key issue for fired managers is to quickly get started on a new job search, for either a comparable position or possibly a new and different career path altogether. If you were following the free agent guidelines, it will be easier because you already know some headhunters and have a network of acquaintances accustomed to thinking of you in connection with new positions. But if you were caught by surprise and are just starting to look around, there is still time to catch up. Make a list of personal and professional interests, and write down an inventory of every talent and skill that might interest a new employer. Then get busy and stay busy.

Start systematically calling every business friend and acquaintance you can think of, including managers whose firms you did business with on behalf of your old employer. Suppliers, consultants, competitors, sales agencies: all of these are logical prospects and will already know you. If your firm was taken over, you may be welcomed by a former competitor, who is better able to appraise and value your experience than the aliens now running your old company.

The crucial importance of being active so soon after the event, and getting the word out immediately, is to force you to become future oriented. What counts now is your future, and you must resist letting the trauma of a firing take your mind over to relive past events, right old wrongs, or wish things could be different. All these thoughts must be removed from your mind so you can concentrate on where you want to be heading rather than on what you are leaving behind. What counts now is your future.

HOW YOUR EX-COMPANY SHOULD HELP YOU.

Both fired managers and their former companies share a common interest in how well the ex-managers do right after leaving employment. Most companies want to see a smooth transition so that those who remain behind become less fearful for their own futures. Also, a smooth transition for those forced to leave helps to combat bad local publicity for the firm, and a bad reputation in management circles outside the company.

As a result, many firms pay back a fraction of the money "saved" from firing their managers by continuing their health benefits for a time after they leave and providing outplacement counseling to help them find new jobs. These benefits are important and concrete signs that your company is willing to follow up on mere words, such as "We're sorry" about your firing or early retirement.

If your company does not offer these exit benefits routinely, you are not out of line if you demand them. This is no time to roll over and be nice to your former employer, and you are still in a negotiating position. If such benefits are not being made available, the company can be forcefully reminded how far it is lagging behind other large employers. In its last survey of how 512 companies handle layoffs and shutdowns, for example, the Conference Board, a prestigious business research organization, found that 79 percent of them extended health-care benefits by as much as one year after termination. Sixty percent operated in-house outplacement programs, while others contracted with professional outplacement counselors on behalf of their employees. And in 88 percent of all the closings reported, advance notice was given, with at least three months' notice provided in over half of them. That was back in 1984, and understates the even greater frequency of these practices since then. With firings so prevalent today, it is not only legitimate but also responsible and proper for managers to expect aid from corporations forcing them out the door.

The most effective way for firms to demonstrate their interest in the well-being of managers they fire is to contract for the services of knowledgeable and experienced outplacement counselors. Many experienced outplacement counselors are former managers who have been through the same degrading experience themselves. They will teach you many things about yourself as they gently help and push you to make your own future jobs and career happen. For many fired managers, professional outplacement counseling has made a world of difference.

The rapid growth of outplacement firms, up more than 300 percent since 1982, is tied directly to the jump in dismissals resulting from corporate restructurings. Outplacement firms are often hired by companies to relieve their guilt and ease the pain that they have inflicted on their managers. These firms provide an important service as a sort of halfway house for fired managers looking for new jobs. Besides giving invaluable counseling, they provide managers with a temporary office to report to each day, complete with phones, secretarial services, and employment manuals. This eases the transition and alleviates much of the stress brought on by unemployment. The cost of such services is usually 10–15 percent of your previous annual salary plus bonuses. Do not hesitate to demand it; you need it and the company owes it to you. The "office" outplacement firms provide will also serve to keep up your professional image. It becomes your business address, substituting for your old company's if you are unable to hold onto space there in the interim.

Managers can provide for themselves several of the key contributions outplacement agencies offer. The essentials are an office and phone outside your home. Looking for work is a regular, full-time job. It is not effectively performed at home, with its built-in distractions and temptation to relax and lounge around. "It's hard enough to get up and get going when you don't have a job. If you don't have somewhere to go, it's very easy to waste your time," says Joseph L. Clark, ex-director of public relations with Kaiser Steel Corporation. At outplacement agencies, in addition to having a new business location, managers also get to meet other competent managers and share their experience of having to make the same set of adjustments.

If you have been given notice but are still employed, try to hold onto the same amenities at the company for as long as possible. Do not move out, even if your company says you can just take the money and leave. Work for yourself by keeping the office as a place to receive mail and messages, and to use for lining up your next job interviews. This is more effective than having no business address, since recruiters will take you more seriously when you have a continuing company affiliation than when you are working from a home address, suggesting you are unemployed. A good in-house model of what employers can provide managers they have fired is the career-continuation office International Harvester set up for managers who became "redundant" when it sold its Agricultural Equipment Division to Tenneco. These fired employees could work at finding another job out of this new "office," and were provided telephone credit cards by the company to further aid in this process.

A second, more psychological service provided by outplacement agencies is to help managers take stock of who they are, what they do best, and what they would like to become. Being fired, paradoxically, is an event that often forces people to get into better touch with themselves. Experienced career counselors ask you to talk about how you see yourself, how you think others see you, what you are like to work with, whom you admire most, and your family and friends. Then, with your permission, they will talk with eight or ten people who have worked for and with you to check out your impressions.

"After three tests and another interview, we integrate all that data and have another discussion usually lasting a couple of hours," explains Joseph Jannotta, chairman of Jannotta Bray & Associates, a Chicago-based outplacement firm, "coming to your strengths, your weaknesses, and really what are the implications for your next job . . . culture, line versus staff, size of company. We put together a strategy, and stay with clients as they go out in the marketplace."

Firings lead to a process of soul-searching that managers do on their own and with close family and friends. "What kind of job do I want to try for?" "Where might we want to move?" are among the questions most often addressed. Career counselors you might hire can also supply both the office facilities and the valuable psychological support provided by outplacement agencies.

A critical question for the fired manager is, who pays for these comprehensive services? Outplacement firms bill the ex-employers of the managers directly and do not charge their manager-clients. The services they provide, as well as continued health benefits, are standard parts of the exit package offered by most corporate employers.

What if your company is not in the majority providing these benefits to ease the transition? If the former employer is refusing help and playing hardball against the managers it pushed out, a consultation with a labor lawyer is a wise investment. He or she will be more knowledgeable and less confused than you about what you can demand and expect from your former company.

A firing or forced resignation is much like a divorce. During the negotiations, much of what happens between you and the firm now is between adversaries and *former* partners. Exit packages are sometimes presented to intimidate or bluff managers into lowering their expectations. Much of what the company tells you follows a script written by its lawyers to discourage you from asking for more and pressure you to accept immediately what is offered. Consulting a lawyer of your own serves as a useful "reality check" on whatever information or misinformation you are being fed. It is very likely, for example, that if you had an employment contract it did not specify what severance arrangements would consist of or state that outplacement assistance (preferably with a firm of your own choosing) would be made available at company expense.

Still, companies are uncomfortable with the thought of your having independent legal counsel, even though they may not make any employee terminations without first consulting their own attorneys. They know management firings and layoffs on today's scale are too new to make easy predictions of how suits against ex-employers for "wrongful discharge" and "libel" will turn out. Where employees have sued companies for balking at legitimate requests, courts have been ruling increasingly *against* the companies. Most states protect employees from being fired "at will," and some are open to the emerging legal doctrine that employment is an implied contract, obliging companies to do more for employees than fire them when they are no longer needed.

As a result, if an attorney contacts your ex-company on your behalf, you may find them willing to negotiate rather than risk costly settlements and bad publicity in the courtroom. Sometimes the lawyer's threat to go public with a strong case is all that is needed to bring the company around to sweetening terms that it claimed earlier were nonnegotiable.

Laws covering firings and exit "windows" vary from state to state, and a good lawyer will tell you when your employer is being fair or when your case is weak. Lawsuits should not be motivated by looking backward to get even. Your focus should be on the future. You should file a lawsuit only if you can make a strong case that your future is being held back by improper actions of questionable legality taken by your ex-employer. Companies' fears of being sued by dismissed employees already have forced many to offer more generous severance packages to departing managers. Companies also have found suits can be avoided if they actively help discharged employees locate new jobs fast.

Being fired is a shocking experience. It should not remain a private affair, kept to yourself. It certainly is not a time to behave like a good soldier or team member toward your ex-company. If you want something you must ask for it, forcefully and up front. You have too much at stake, financially and psychologically, to just "take it" politely. If you are in a "protected" category, such as being older, female, physically handicapped, or from a minority group, your lawyer should be able to determine if a class

class action suit is applicable. Unless you have a good professional reason for remaining quiet, and can realistically assume people won't know what happened anyway, you have no reason to leave holding a vow of silence.

Years after the firing of Grace Keaton as described in chapter 3, she still regretted not having talked with a lawyer immediately after she was let go. Nearly everyone who is fired shares her inability to think straight when they first get the news. Although there is no guarantee that seeing a lawyer will change things, you won't have to wonder for years afterward, "Should I have sued?" You will have learned what you can or cannot receive in compensation, and also have competent counsel available for any future job prospects and inquiries.

Just as the wise Free Agent Manager stays on good terms with headhunters, knowing a good lawyer further rounds out your own team and support group. The cost of maintaining such casual relationships is not high and clearly worth the investment. Learning that a lump-sum severance settlement paid out in annual installments may cost you less in taxes than when it is all paid out at once, for example, is important information to have at your fingertips. Having these experienced professionals on call, including a good accountant to guide you through the complex thicket of tax law, new perks, benefits, and complex balance sheets, all help in making a clean break from the last job and better preparing you for the next leg of your journey.

6. Managers in the 1990s

The Nineties will see a focus on materialism, "a desire to get it now because we are unsure of where we are headed."

prediction by Ann Clurman, for market forecaster Yankelovich Clancy Shulman

Forecasters have finally realized that restructurings and downsizings are forcing managers to feel like an endangered species. What further challenges should managers expect to face in the 1990s? How should you plan your free agent strategies to meet them? And what new developments should you take into account when deciding to which new job opportunities you should commit?

The 1990s will be a decade of increasingly transient employment relationships. This will affect how patient you should be about waiting for pensions to become vested, and for salaries and benefits to go up. Managers will seek and get more employment contracts with explicit provisions covering matters previously handled informally over handshakes. More managers will become self-employed, or hire out on a temporary basis to work on staff projects for companies that no longer handle the assignments in-house. Project consulting firms, and even more "Office Temporary" agencies offering an expanded range of services, including accountants and other skilled managers, will spring up to broker such arrangements.

In the midst of these changes, managers should anticipate a period of rough sledding. If things are going to get worse before they get better, you must increase your own odds of coming out ahead. Alongside the earlier themes, "Get Ready to Leave" and "Be Streetsmart and Realistic," Free Agent Managers should now add "Get It While You Can!" For until America's financial markets permit corporations to plan for the long term rather than be milked as short-run cash cows, managers should not expect any improvement in the reliability of our biggest employers. Career ladders within firms will remain limited, and the importance of following free agent strategies such as maintaining visibility, marketability, and credibility will become even more critical.

Short-Term Employment

The 1990s will see a movement to loosen corporate reserve clauses traditionally used to bind managers by withholding accumulated benefits if they move on to maintain mobility. Since corporations have lowered their commitment to employees, Free Agent Managers increasingly look for companies honest enough to let them choose when to leave, without losing pension monies and deferred bonuses that do not kick in unless you stay ten years or longer. Indeed, while programs with vested portions that disappear if you leave one year early discriminate against all managers, they are most consistently loaded against younger employees in today's cold business climate. Firing should be a two-way street.

Most pensions and deferred profit-sharing plans were not set up with restructurings in mind. They should be replaced by a system of portable pensions, where managers can transfer what they have earned to the next firm's equivalent account, or a private IRA-type fund rollover. When companies announce how unlikely it is that today's younger employees will still be working there when they retire, it is time for the companies to reduce or eliminate the vesting period. Free Agent Managers will push for "defined contribution" plans that relax this time requirement as well as provide employees more options for setting up this important benefit.

Vested pension plans work against managers two more ways in the era of restructurings. First, they encourage an employer to keep your salary below your market value, for it knows managers are unlikely to move if it means losing benefits accrued over a long time period. And second, most managers have probably already lost what used to be near-automatic cost of living increases in the pension payments paid by your company to employees once they do retire. These were drawn from the "overfunded" portion of pension plans, those millions of dollars placed in the account by corporations, but not legally required to be there. During the 1980s, Wall Street and corporate raiders declared these funds part of the victor's spoils in a takeover or restructuring. As a result, many corporations withdrew these contributions and ended their voluntary increases to the pensions of retired employees.

The message from each of these pension-related horror stories, once again, is that you no longer can count on your company to be there for you when you need it later on down the road. In the new world of short-term employment, "getting it while you can" means charging your full market value when you are needed, keeping mobile, and staying visible in the marketplace. When you know you have more than one job to choose from and do not desperately need either position, don't hesitate to ask for more money, responsibility, or promises in writing than you might otherwise feel comfortable asking for.

Free agents seek out such attractive situations. As we approach the 1990s, human resource experts expect this perspective will soon become the new norm followed by both managers and their employers. "Where companies . . . find they cannot afford to [provide lifetime employment]," says Mary Ann Devanna, of Columbia University's Career Research Center, compensation will become "front-end loaded." That is, managers will receive higher salaries earlier, but with no promises about a lifetime career with the company.

Middle Age More Hazardous

Over the next ten years, the populous and ambitious baby-boom generation will be pressing for promotion in the middle ranks just as those middle ranks are reduced, particularly in large companies.

"The Economy of the 1990's," a Special Report in *Fortune*, 1987

"So many managers have been demoted, there is a layer on top of me—people in their 40's and 50's that I will never get through," says one 30-year-old employee. "For the survivors there are no opportunities. Moving up is a thing of the past." For this employee and others like her, Exxon simply has become a way station to a better job.

"The End of Corporate Loyalty?", in *Business Week*, 1986

About the only age group not seriously threatened by the growing recession in attractive jobs for middle managers is the under-thirty, entry-level population. Young managers in this group have the least to lose because they are farthest away from the promotions that are drying up. They have been with their companies for the shortest time, have more time to adjust, and are still more mobile and resilient. Having salaries lower than managers above them is beneficial when it comes to getting a new position and helps to further reduce their "down time" between jobs.

For managers forty or older, life is becoming reminiscent of the old Chinese curse "May your life be interesting." With cutbacks in corporate positions more and more widespread, uncertainty is rising to new heights. While this presents new opportunities, strategies such as be prepared to scramble, follow free agent guidelines, and expect the unexpected are becoming more important to retaining control over your own world and peace of mind.

Managers in their forties are especially vulnerable to corporate upheavals. This is the age when new houses and condominiums are purchased, children's schools selected, and other serious commitments taken on. It is the most likely age to have just celebrated doing well on the job by taking on heavy financial obligations. These are often based on the clear sailing many are told they can look forward to at the company. When the downsizing or restructuring hits shortly afterward, it is a crushing blow, especially for the many who had no parachute packed. Severance and retirement arrangements, up to age fifty-five, are unlikely to be large enough to keep dismissed managers solvent for very long.

If you are in this age category and work in a big corporation, protect yourself by learning what other jobs are available elsewhere. Make shop-talking with many people, inside and out of your firm, a normal part of your work life, and be willing to give serious thought to interesting alternatives with attractive futures. Also stay alert to what's happening on your company's financial side, and to information about how its shares are doing in the stock market. Pay careful attention to where you and your company place on the individual job and company risk profiles.

Taking these actions will not mean you are bailing out of your job prematurely. Getting into the habit of knowing where the jobs are and how big a risk your company is running with investors simply keeps you in touch with the outside world on which your future career will very likely depend. In the 1990s, for example, most new jobs will be with small and growing businesses, not large corporations. They are worth looking into and adding to the list of possibilities you have checked out, whether you are happily employed now or out looking for new work.

While managers in their forties are wise to trade up from positions offering little chance of advancement, managers over fifty will find a wider range of choices in the 1990s. If you have been with the company a long time and are then demoted or "red circled," but not dismissed, what should you do? Your choice here leaves more room for personal considerations, such as your present energy level, the degree of your financial need and indignation, and the amount of creature comforts remaining at the familiar company you already know. All these come into play when there are major changes afoot. One option you may have that younger managers should avoid is to hang in there anyway, to "cash it in" by "disinvesting" your emotional energy and commitment from the firm, while still remaining on the payroll. When the choice remains theirs, some older managers decide they'd rather spend more time with family and friends and on their own interests rather than start over somewhere else.

Others decide to leave, or have this decision made for them. If you are a fired long-service manager over fifty, there is both good and bad news about the job world you now face. First, the bad news: a dismissal or unwanted retirement at this later stage of your career generally packs a much stronger emotional wallop than if you were still an up-and-coming younger manager. Much more of you is invested in your company. Even worse, you probably have not had to look for work in years, and have heard that corporations prefer hiring younger, cheaper managers whom they can train, promote, and control more easily.

The good news, paradoxically, comes from the same trends toward restructuring that put you back on the job market in the first place. "With companies [no longer] expecting people to remain in their employ for an indefinite time, age makes little difference in the newly hired and youth loses its advantage," notes Chicago outplacement consultant James Challenger. During the 1990s, companies will not be interested in hiring and developing as many young managers for the long run, since corporate commitments are moving toward specific projects and product needs with shorter time horizons. Ironically, the advantages once held by youthful managers competing against you for new jobs fade away when the company has less interest in developing or keeping new hirees of any age for very long.

Once these positions are no longer training routes for fast-track promotions and long-term relationships, seasoned pros coming in with experience look much more attractive. They require less training than new graduates and are less likely to mind leaving in a few years. This may result in more companies investing in "sheer wisdom rather than sheer energy," concludes Mr. Challenger. Additional opportunities for older managers will also emerge as these younger, energetic managers fall off the disappearing single-company corporate ladder. During the 1990s, many of them will start up new businesses that need help from the wisdom, experience, contacts, and perspective older managers can provide.

While the big corporation will be hiring fewer managers at any age and will stay hard to crack for older managers, their marketability is improving for overflow and offshoot positions in the managerial work force. Explosions in the number of short-term staff projects big companies award outside consultants, and in new business start-ups and management assignments through office temporary firms, all provide employment while managers regroup their forces and decide what to do next. Such contract jobs, notes the University of Chicago's Richard Thain, can be especially appealing to managers "who have found themselves stranded by mergers, acquisitions, buyouts, takeovers, and plain misfortune at the higher ages." For managers of all ages, but especially older ones better able to withstand ups and downs in their monthly income, becoming an independent contractor or consultant is an increasingly common solution for the interim, or even the long-term if it results in a stable clientele or a full-time position.

Entrepreneurship and Starting Your Own Business

Free Agent Managers break the stereotype that sees corporate life and entrepreneurial thinking as worlds apart. In fact, any manager following free agent strategies is already doing a fine job as an entrepreneurial businessman or -woman as well. Whether housed in large corporations, hiring out as independent contractors, or owning and operating their own businesses, Free Agent Managers have a keen understanding of their market, will pick up and go whenever opportunity knocks, make good on their promises, maintain visibility, and know whom to call when they need help or advice. When they take a plunge into small business, they do not burn their bridges back to the corporate world. Instead, free agents retain their ties to headhunters and former associates, keeping alive their choice between work environments. As careers in the 1990s zigzag a bit more, becoming less predictable and smooth, some Free Agent Managers will switch back and forth regularly between these different types of jobs and companies.

Over the next decade, the number of new jobs in service industries such as finance and communications will greatly outnumber the growth of new jobs in the manufacturing sector. A wide range of professional services will also be expanding, ranging from public relations and advertising to law, research, and even engineering. These are precisely the areas in which corporations, in their frenzy to become lean and mean, have already made the steepest cuts. Some large employers, such as DuPont, had to hire back their ex-managers as high-priced consultants after so many responded to company incentives to leave that the organization couldn't run smoothly without them. To retrieve many of the in-house activities they threw out, companies that restructured will be heavy users of consultants and more frequent customers of companies marketing the very services that these clients just axed. Other activities suffering the same fate in the 1980s, such as maintenance, repair work, and food service, will also rise anew through outside contracting.

A growth area for the 1990s will be the organization, marketing, and administration of these many new freestanding services. If you think you may be among the thousands of ex-corporate managers joining or starting a small business of your own, free agent guidelines will come in very handy in helping you decide how to proceed.

Going off on your own puts you in an exhilarating and scary new world, bringing great new highs and lows. But the decision to get off the more standard career train is a weighty one that should not be treated lightly. To jump into a completely new venture on an impulsive rebound from nasty treatment by your last employer would be a mistake. To start a new venture requires even more carefully thought-out advance planning than corporate free agents engage in before taking a new but similar job at another large company. In the panic atmosphere surrounding surprise restructurings, a few words of caution also are in order.

If you have not had prior experience in smaller and noncorporate situations before, you should be prepared in advance to answer such questions as:

> How familiar are you with the people and products or services you will soon be depending on?
>
> Will you have an ownership stake if you are joining someone else's small business?
>
> How much of your time and money are you willing to invest?

The success of new ventures is enhanced when you start out knowing a great deal about your product or service and the customers and supplies you will be dealing with. This seems obvious, but it is amazing how many managers become so giddy at the thought of finally running their own show that they forget this simple fact of business life. This knowledge of product and customer can follow from what you already learned on the job while working for big companies in related areas, or from advance research you conduct part-time, preferably while still on somebody else's payroll. It is much harder to "earn while you learn" if you are starting out from scratch on your own time and money. If a new venture's product idea follows a personal interest, such as a hobby you have pursued for years, the problem of not knowing enough about the product and some of the industry's main players is lessened.

Today's most successful entrepreneurs bring valuable types of experience with them *before* they plunge into a new world of smaller ventures. Ross Perot was a superstar at IBM before founding his enormously successful Electronic Data Services (EDS), for example. Victor Kiam, the clean-shaven owner of Remington Products Company, familiar to many from his television commercials for its electric shavers, bought the company in a fire sale after working for two premier consumer marketing companies, Playtex and Lever Brothers. While he says he bought Remington because he "liked the razor so much," his advice to would-be entrepreneurs emphasizes the importance of prior experience for success with any new venture.

These successful entrepreneurs did not start their firms on a wild impulse. They had the free agent's traits of credibility in their professions before starting out, with a track record of previous accomplishments and visibility.

All of these tools from years of prior experience help explain Leo J. LeBlanc's success as a new owner after being fired as a vice president at Rockwell International. LeBlanc located a declining company, invested most of his life savings, and turned around Brass Works, Inc., within months. His explanation:

> I knew quickly when I walked through the plant what they were doing wrong because that had been my field of expertise for years. I got in some good people who knew what to do. Rockwell did me a favor.

Mr. LeBlanc's success as an entrepreneur was aided by his maintaining enough generality to know how to improve his new product. Following free agent strategies, he also maintained his networks with enough visibility to know who to call on for help in getting the new venture off the ground. His expertise and contacts from the years at Rockwell also contributed strongly to his impressive success with a new venture. He did an excellent job of packing his own parachute.

There will be great opportunities for new business start-ups during the 1990s. Entrepreneurial activity will skyrocket in the growing service sector, alongside ventures like Mr. LeBlanc's in more traditional industries. Still more opportunities in high technology and other areas will arise as fewer innovations emerge from Fortune 500 companies that drove talent away and stopped funding new projects during the cost-cutting orgy of the 1980s.

At the same time, the risks entailed by abandoning the corporate world for new business start-ups remain substantial. On the other side of the glory, money, and great personal satisfaction from successful new ventures is the substantial risk that the gamble may not pay off. Whether the new venture being considered is large or small, management expert Peter Drucker's summary of why experience counts for so much applies to both:

> The most successful of the young entrepreneurs today are people who have spent five to eight years in a big organization. They learn. They get tools. They learn cash-flow analysis and how one trains people and how one delegates and how one builds a team. I know a good many of them and the strength of practically all of them is that they have five or ten years of, call it, management under their

> belts before they start. If you don't have it then you make asinine mistakes.

The importance of gaining experience before setting out on your own is underscored by an unusual statistic on new business start-ups. Prior experience is so important that if, say, two entrepreneurs open up equivalent businesses on the same day, the one who failed earlier in a new venture is now the more likely one to succeed, benefiting from the previous experience.

Learning from the earlier experience, even if it failed, provides an advantage the second time around. Although such warnings have never stopped the adventurous, they may give pause to others feeling undecided, fainthearted, or strapped for cash. They also might encourage anyone who failed once before to try again.

Entrepreneurial Free Agent Managers play hard and seek to push back the limits. Managers with the most staying power set higher goals for themselves than can be easily achieved, but they also pull back when their goals are blocked rather than let temporary setbacks stop them cold. Free agents keep their eyes on the *next* contest rather than let today's struggle absorb all their attention. This is the correct stance toward a corporate world that devalues managers and takes orders from stock markets fixated only on the short-term gain.

Against these restraints, managers need to retain the edge provided by free agent guidelines and having their parachutes packed at all times. This advice follows the tradition laid down by a wise man who once noticed that the harder he worked, the luckier he got. If you are thinking of leaving your current job, or have been told to go, you should be sorting out professional and personal life-style questions, such as what type of company you wish to be with next. More personally, you should evaluate what career stage you are in and how much of your time you want to put into the next job.

Free agent guidelines are designed to help you seize opportunities when they arise and to know when you are in the right place at the right time to do so. Successful careers have to be planned and worked at, opportunities located and acted upon. Being able to take charge is a wonderful feeling when it works out. It is the occupational world we are all seeking.

For occasions when things do not go swimmingly, remember you are in excellent company, all across the land. With downsizings and other setbacks potentially around every corner, take to heart the four words of advice given to his troops by the sergeant on television's "Hill Street Blues" during nearly every week of the turbulent 1980s: "Be Careful Out There." And keep trying!

Notes

Abbreviations:
BW = *Business Week*
WSJ = *Wall Street Journal*
NYT = *New York Times*

PREFACE

P. xv *Inside Corporate America,* New York: St. Martin's (1986).

P. xv *Confessions of a Corporate Headhunter,* New York: Trident (1973).

P. xv "to make money." In "The Raiders: 'They Are Really Breaking the Vise of the Managing Class,'" *BW* (3/4/85), p. 81.

P. xv "to make money." William Gruber, "Raider Carl Icahn—a pirate or a patriot?" *Chicago Tribune* (5/12/85), Sect. 7, p. 1.

P. xv "to make money." Allan Sloan, "Why is No One Safe?" *Forbes* (3/11/85), p. 140.

P. xvi "is my purse." Connie Bruck, "My Master is My Purse," *Atlantic Monthly* (12/84), p. 96.

INTRODUCTION. All unattributed quotes in this section come from interviews arranged and conducted by Dr. Dennis Wheaton, a native of Whizbang, Oklahoma, an abandoned boomtown located fifty miles west of Bartlesville in the Burbank Field of Osage County.

P. 1 "wells in the U.S." Tim Hartley, "Conflicting Signals: Phillips reductions complete but home sales continue strong," *Bartlesville Examiner-Enterprise* (8/4/86), p. 2.

P. 1 "house in Bartlesville." Personal interview (7/86).

P. 1 "couldn't get one." Tim Hartley, op. cit., p. 1.

P. 2 "to be next?" David Clark Scott, "Although raid at Phillips is over, the company is the poorer," *Christian Science Monitor* (3/12/85), p. 21.

P. 2 "someone who is." In Sallie Turcott, "Phillips Workers Wait for Bad News," *Tulsa World* (4/4/86), p. D-1.

P. 2 "that's no joke." John Williams and Charles McCoy, "Phillips, Icahn Set Pact to Halt Takeover Effort," *WSJ* (3/5/85), p. 20.

P. 2 "for the money." Personal interview (7/86).

P. 3 "a tough situation." Personal interview (7/86).

P. 3 "through your town?" Personal interview (7/86).

P. 4 "were running separately." Personal interview (10/86).

P. 4 "is still intact." Personal interview (10/86).

P. 4 "could use [them!]". "Odds & Ends," *WSJ* (4/11/85), Section 2, p. 1.

P. 4 "don't like it." "Bartlesville Is Wary," *NYT* (2/6/85), p. 29.

P. 5 "let's do it!" *Bartlesville Constitution: Extra* (12/14/84), p. 3.

P. 5 "come to Bartlesville." Personal interview (10/86).

P. 6 "profit he did." Personal interview (10/86).

P. 6 "to its future." Daniel Cuff, "Hometown Fights for Phillips," *NYT* (2/11/85), p. D1.

P. 7 "happens to Bartlesville." In "Icahn Moves to Block Phillips Plan," *Bartlesville Constitution* (2/6/85), p. 1.

P. 7 "too,' he said." Scott Andrews, "Douce: Phillips has other options," *Bartlesville Examiner-Enterprise* (2/28/85), p. 1.

P. 7 "was Mr. SOB." Personal interview (7/86).

P. 7 "who he is?" Personal interview (7/86).

P. 7 "improved the terms." Robert J. Cole, "Icahn Ends Offer for Phillips; All Shareholders to Get More," *NYT* (3/5/85), p. 1.

P. 8 "put up a nickel." Moira Johnston, *Takeover: The New Wall Street Warriors.* New York: Arbor House (1986), p. 151.

P. 8 "rest easy tonight." Robert J. Cole, op. cit., p. D9.

P. 8 "describes the mood," David Clark Scott, op. cit.

P. 8 "fights dragged on." Personal interview (7/86).

P. 9 "have a job." David Clark Scott, "How citizens and businesses rally round when a takeover threat strides into town," *Christian Science Monitor* (4/22/85), p. 14.

P. 9 "$2 billion without blinking." John Williams and Charles McCoy, "Phillips is expected to retain its current shape even after planned sale of $2 billion in assets," *WSJ* (3/6/85), p. 2.

P. 9 "name of the game." Daniel Cuff, "Phillips Sees Benefits in Fight; Others Unsure," *NYT* (3/6/85), p. D1.

P. 9 "born-again debtor." Mark Potts, "Phillips Offers Blueprint for Industry Change," *Washington Post* (3/17/85), p. D8.

P. 9 "vital, no question." John Williams and Charles McCoy, op. cit.

P. 9 "mountain of debt." David Clark Scott, op. cit.

P. 9 "glow has been extinguished." Daniel Cuff, op. cit.

P. 10 "Pickens attacked them." In "Shifting Strategies: Surge in Restructuring is Profoundly Altering Much of U.S. Industry" (Special Report), *WSJ* (8/12/85), p. 12.

P. 10 "75 percent debt." Mark Potts, "Does Another Oil Shock Lie Ahead?", *Washington Post* (5/5/85), p. F20.

P. 10 "$20 a barrel." Mark Potts, "Phillips Offers Blueprint For Industry Change," *Washington Post*, op. cit., p. D1.

P. 10 "be in trouble." David C. Scott, op. cit.

P. 10 "faced financial peril." Daniel Cuff, "Phillips Sees Benefits in Fight; Others Unsure," op. cit.

P. 11 "biggest oil company." Laurie Cohen and Johnathan Dahl, "Phillips Is Pressured by Debt, Oil-Pride Slide," *WSJ* (8/9/85), p. 6.

P. 12 "first of the year." Frederick Rose and Karen Blumenthal, "Heavy Debts Weigh on Unocal, Phillips," *WSJ* (7/28/86), p. 6.

P. 12 "look like hell." Laurie Cohen and Johnathan Dahl, op. cit.

P. 12 "continue as we are." Personal interview (10/86).

P. 12 "much as possible." Personal interview (7/86).

P. 12 "slimming the . . . payroll." In "Shifting Strategies: Surge in Restructuring . . . ," op. cit.

P. 12 "cutting dividends further." Frederick Rose and Karen Blumenthal, op. cit.

P. 13 "destroyed a part of." Personal interview (10/86).

P. 13 "cutting entity." David Clark Scott, "How citizens and businesses rally round when takeover threat strides into town," op. cit.

P. 13 "type of development." Daniel Cuff, "Phillips Sees Benefits in Fight; Others Unsure," op. cit.

CHAPTER 1

P. 21 "or even thanks. Damn!" Taken from personal interviews (4/85–6/85).

P. 23 "corpocracy." Term coined by former Deputy U.S. Treasury Secretary Richard Darman in November 1986.

P. 25 "corporations they run." Steven Prokesh, "Executives Favor Curbs on 'Raiders,'" *NYT* (11/21/86), p. 24.

P. 25 "benefits to shareholders now." Daniel Cuff, "Phillips Sees Benefits in Fight; Others Unsure," op. cit.

P. 25 "has been diminished." Daniel Cuff, "Hometown Fights for Phillips," op. cit.

P. 27 "the company's constituents." Jay Lorsch, "In Defense of the Corporate Defender," *NYT* (5/20/84), p. F3.

P. 27 "[is] dangerous." Warren Law, "A Corporation Is More Than Its Stock," *Harvard Business Review* (May–June 1986), p. 81.

P. 28 "next week's stock price." In "Manic Market," *Time* (11/10/86), p. 66.

P. 28 "in their charge. . . ." Peter Drucker, "Taming the Corporate Takeover," *WSJ* (10/30/84), p. 30.

P. 28 "for the short term." Peter Drucker, "Corporate Takeovers—What Is to Be Done?" *The Public Interest* (Winter 1986), p. 16.

P. 29 *Theory Z: How American Business Can Meet the Japanese Challenge*. Reading, Mass.: Addison-Wesley (1981).

P. 29 *In Search of Excellence: Lessons from America's Best-Run Companies*. New York: Harper & Row (1982).

P. 29 "more *responsive* structure." In "Ease the Hardship of Layoffs," *BW* (8/4/86), p. 84.

P. 30 "anything beyond that." Felix Kessler, "Managers Without a Company," *Fortune* (10/28/85), p. 52.

P. 30 "health or family problems." Myron Magnet, "Help! My Company Has Just Been Taken Over," *Fortune* (7/9/84), p. 44.

P. 31 "they're horrendous." William M. Carley, "Carl Icahn's Strategies in His Quest for TWA Are a Model for Raiders," *WSJ* (6/20/85), p. 24.

P. 31 "—the gardeners." Michael VerMuelen, "Who's Afraid of Carl Icahn? Who Isn't?" *TWA Ambassador* (9/84).

P. 31 "to a takeover." *U.S. News & World Report* (8/22/85), p. 57.

P. 31 "assets work best." Ibid.

P. 31 "in the marketplace." Warren Law, op. cit., p. 81.

P. 31 "baboons in Africa." "High Times for T. Boone Pickens," *Time* (3/4/85), p. 53.

P. 33 "they canned us." Isadore Barmesh, *Welcome to Our Conglomerate—You're Fired!* New York: Grosset & Dunlap (1971), p. xii.

P. 35 "this community. . . ." "Carl Icahn: Raider or Manager?" *BW* (10/27/86), p. 98.

P. 35 "the downtown area." Ibid., p. 104.

P. 35 "ACF Industries, Inc." "Icahn has USX Boxed In," *BW* (10/20/86), p. 24.

P. 36 "Pittsburgh Chamber of Commerce." Mark Russell, *WSJ* (10/9/86), p. 7.

P. 36 "whole [Esmark] departments." Sally Hodge, "In Mergers, Ethics Aren't a Part of the Deal," *Chicago Tribune* (9/3/85), p. 3.

P. 37 "going to see." In "Shifting Strategies . . . ," *WSJ*, op. cit., p. 1.

P. 38 "have enough notice." Personal interview (8/85).

P. 41 "return to shareholders." In "Do All These Deals Help or Hurt the U.S. Economy?" *BW* (11/24/86), p. 88.

P. 42 "consider bad management." In "More Than Ever,

It's Management for the Short Term," *BW* (11/24/86), p. 92.

P. 42 "to 40,000 employees." Warren Law, op. cit., p. 82.

P. 44 "for six months." Art Buchwald, "Tale of Survival in the Takeover Jungle," *Los Angeles Times* (7/11/85), part V, p. 3.

P. 45 "put into job creation." In "More Than Ever: It's Management for the Short Term," op. cit., p. 93.

P. 45 "long-term implications." Leslie Wayne, "How Restructurings Can Help," *NYT* (1/20/86), p. D10.

P. 45 "dog in heat." In "More Than Ever: It's Management for the Short Term," op. cit., p. 93.

P. 45 "Goldman Sachs & Co." Ann Kates, "Corporate Deals Pay Off for Investors," *USA Today* (1/27/86), p. E1.

P. 46 "at a torrid pace." Herb Greenberg, "The Wailing Wall: Boesky case has financial community in a dither," *Chicago Tribune* (11/23/86), p. C9.

P. 47 "or undergoing a restructuring." John Crudele, "Pond's Stock Rises $4 a Share," *NYT* (11/29/86), p. 37.

P. 47 "would be acquired." Ibid.

P. 47 "jungle of Wall Street," Ralph Winter, "Myopic Managers? Trying to Streamline Some Firms May Hurt Long-Term Prospects," *WSJ* (1/8/87), p. 10.

P. 48 "[raider] Victor Posner." In "The Raiders: They Are Really Breaking the Vise of the Managing Class," *BW*, op. cit., p. 90.

P. 48 "as the raiders." Ibid.

P. 48 "not doing his job." In "Shifting Strategies: Surge in Restructuring Is Profoundly Altering Much of U.S. Industry," op. cit., p. 1.

P. 48 "personally had fired." Richard Gibson, "Minstar's Jacobs to Sell AMF Businesses; Most of Corporate Staff Has Been Fired," *WSJ* (8/30/85), p. 22.

P. 48 "only about 50." Ibid.

P. 48 "like a cemetery." Winston Williams, "A Raider Takes Command at AMF," *NYT* (9/1/85), p. 22f.

P. 48 "winners." In Richard Gibson, op. cit. See also "Jacobs Loses No Time at AMF," *BW* (9/16/85), p. 38.

P. 49 "with reckless abandon." In "More Than Ever, It's Management for the Short Term," op. cit., p. 93.

P. 50 "drastic cutbacks," Johnathan Hicks, "Goodyear's Uneasy Aftermath," *NYT* (12/5/86), p. D3.

P. 50 "need for cash," Ralph E. Winter and Gregory Stricharchuk, "Goodyear Could Be More Efficient Firm As It Focuses on Tires and Cuts Costs," *WSJ* (11/24/86), p. 4.

P. 50 "plan and shrinks." Ibid.

P. 50 "several times a day. . . ." Hicks, op. cit., pp. 35–36.

P. 50 "leading-edge research." "Goodyear may have lost the war in winning takeover battle," *Chicago Tribune* (11/23/86), section 7, p. 6.

CHAPTER 2

P. 51 "operating the company." In "Do Mergers Really Work?" *BW* (6/3/85), p. 91.

P. 51 "with a meat ax." In Lawrence Ingrassia, "Employees at Acquired Firms Find White Knights Often Unfriendly," *WSJ* (7/7/82), p. 21.

P. 52 "only shades of gray." Ibid.

P. 52 Isadore Barmash, op. cit.

P. 52 "day after the merger." Ingrassia, op. cit.

P. 52 "been committed against us." Myron Magnet, op. cit., p. 44.

P. 53 "to be destroyed." In "Why Gulf Lost Its Fight for Life," *BW* (3/19/84), p. 81.

P. 55 "part of your life." In "People Pay the Highest Price in a Takeover," *U.S. News & World Report* (7/22/85), p. 51.

P. 55 "would have been like." Ken Wells and Carol Hymowitz, "Takeover Trauma: Gulf's Managers Find Merger Into Chevron Forces Many Changes," *WSJ* (12/4/84), p. 22.

P. 56 "worried that they will." Ibid., pp. 1, 22.

P. 58 "can be bagged." "Why Gulf Lost Its Fight for Life," op. cit., p. 77.

P. 59 "largely unproductive." Robert Reich, "A people-based economy," *Christian Science Monitor* (9/19/86), p. 13.

P. 59 "years to turn profitable." Ralph Winter, op. cit., p. 1.

P. 61 "Ewing of 'Dallas.'" In "Turner Nearing Takeover Bid for CBS?" *Chicago Tribune* (4/4/85), section 3, p. 3.

P. 62 "public interest." Sally Bedell Smith, "Paley Sees a 'Tragedy' in a Hostile Shift at CBS," *NYT* (5/1/85), p. 29.

P. 62 "in the 20th Century." Myron Magnet, op. cit., p. 44.

P. 63 "never seen before." Diane Mermigas, "Taking Its Toll: Tisch Takeover Talk Causing Turmoil at CBS," *Electronic Media* (8/18/86), p. 1.

P. 63 "right of first refusal." In "News Media: Hard Money, Hard Times," *Newsweek* (11/4/85), p. 68.

P. 63 "get rid of the rest." In "Can Corporate America Cope?" *Newsweek* (11/17/86), p. 65.

P. 64 "at least as smart." In "Say It Ain't So, Larry," *NYT* (3/21/87), p. 15.

P. 64 "compromised by accountants." Diane Mermigas, "The CBS Cuts: Fat or Muscle?", *Electronic Media* (3/16/87), p. 55.

P. 64 "it is also a business." Ibid.

P. 64 "on the network's behalf." Craig Leddy and Diane Mermigas, "CBS Chief Launches PR Effort," *Electronic Media* (3/23/87). p. 1.

P. 66 "investing in heavy equipment." In "The End of Corporate Loyalty?", *BW* (8/4/86), p. 49.

P. 66 "psychological and physical harm." Robert I. Sutton, Reginald A. Bruce, and Stanley G. Harris, "Epilogue" to special issue on organizational decline, *Human Resource Management* (Winter 1983), p. 468.

P. 67 "their bottom line." Kathleen Teltsch, "Corporate Pressure Slowing Gifts to Charity." *NYT* (7/8/87), p. 1.

P. 67 "rape" and "absolute betrayal." In "What Are Mergers Doing to America?", *U.S. News & World Report* (7/22/85), p. 49.

P. 68 "right here in Pittsburgh." Thomas O'Boyle and Susan Carey, "Gulf's Departing Pittsburgh Would Deal a Harsh Blow to City's Economy and Pride," *WSJ* (3/9/84), p. 33.

P. 69 Pat Choate and J. K. Linger, *The High-Flex Society: Shaping America's Economic Future.* New York: Knopf (1986).

P. 69 "to fight Japan." In "Do All These Deals Help or Hurt the U.S. Economy?", *BW* (11/24/86), p. 86.

P. 69 "thousands of workers?" Ibid., p. 87.

P. 69 "[driven into] oblivion." Peter Nulty, "The Economy of the 1990's: How Managers Will Manage," *Fortune* (2/2/87), p. 47.

CHAPTER 3

P. 71 "be among them." Felix Kessler, "Managers Without a Company." *Fortune* (10/28/85), p. 54.

P. 71 "no longer exists." Ibid.

P. 71 "love with a company once." Personal interview (3/86).

P. 71 "he get paid?" "In "High Times for T. Boone Pickens," *Time* (3/4/85), p. 61.

P. 71 "piece of fruit." Willie Loman in Arthur Miller, *Death of a Salesman*, act II. New York: Penguin Books (1977).

P. 74 "of the company." Personal interview (7/85).

P. 74 "in the country." Personal interview (6/85).

P. 75 "and my career." Felix Kessler, op. cit.

P. 75 "last November." Ibid., p. 56.

P. 78 "just total wipeout." Harry Maurer, *Not Working: An Oral History of the Unemployed*. New York: Holt, Rinehart & Winston (1979), pp. 17–21.

P. 79 "us less alone." Ibid., p. 1.

P. 79 "people blame themselves." Ibid.

P. 80 "into something else." A fired manager quoted in Myron Magnet, op. cit., p. 45.

P. 80 "stress scale." In Dennis Organ and W. Clay Hamner, *Organizational Behavior*. Plano, Tex.: Business Publications (1982), p. 255.

P. 81 "the following year." Ibid.

P. 85 "years to come." Indianapolis: Bobbs-Merrill (1969), pp. 10, 179–80, 303, 322–25. Reissued by the Institute for Social Research, the University of Michigan, Ann Arbor.

P. 86 "going to happen." In "The End of Company Loyalty?", op. cit., p. 49.

P. 88 "lose their shirts." Personal interview (10/86).
P. 89 "kinds of things. Personal interview (1/86).
P. 90 "among their members." Interview with Dr. Rick Gilkey (9/86). For more information, see his *Joining Forces* (co-authored with Dr. Joe McCann). Boston: Ballinger (1987).
P. 90 "a telephone conversation." Dennis Organ and W. Clay Hamner, op. cit., p. 272.
P. 91 "nervous and upset." Personal interview (9/85).
P. 92 "I wasn't fired." Personal interview (6/86).
P. 92 "find out his name." Personal interview (8/85).
P. 92 "side of waste?" "Managing a Downsized Operation," *Fortune* (7/22/85), pp. 155, 160.
P. 93 "terrified." Personal interview (11/86).
P. 93 "cutback brings on." Walter Kiechel III, op. cit.
P. 93 "scared to death." Steven Prokesch, "People Trauma in Mergers," *NYT* (11/19/85), p. 29.
P. 95 "is no involvement." Personal interview (6/86).
P. 95 "long-term instability." Felix Kessler, op. cit., p. 52.
P. 96 "those who remain." Thomas O'Boyle, "Loyalty Ebbs at Many Companies as Employees Grow Disillusioned," *WSJ* (7/11/85), p. 25.
P. 96 "a favorable rating." Steven Prokesh, "People Trauma in Mergers," op. cit., pp. 29, 33.
P. 96 "not about to end." In "The End of Corporate Loyalty?", op. cit., p. 49.
P. 96 "It hurts too much." Personal interview (3/86).
P. 98 "from me again." Ibid.
P. 99 "heart and soul." Felix Kessler, op. cit., p. 54.
P. 99 "personal feelings anymore." Jeanne Dorin McDowell, "The Demise of Loyalty," *NYT* (3/3/85), p. F1.
P. 100 "afraid to take chances." Felix Kessler, op. cit.
P. 100 "can't understand it." Edward Atorino in "News Update," *TV Guide* (11/9/85), p. A2.
P. 101 "from me again." Personal interview (3/86).
P. 101 "than it's ever been." Thomas O'Boyle, "Loyalty Ebbs at Many Companies as Employees Grow Disillusioned," op. cit.
P. 101 "mergers, and layoffs." Ibid.

P. 102	"ideal employer." *The Mobile Manager*, Research Report, Heidrick & Struggles, Inc., Chicago (1985), pp. 1, 13, 14.

CHAPTER 4

P. 107	"count on yourself." Letter in *Fortune* (11/25/85), p. 11.
P. 107	"That's its job." Edward F. Mrkvicka, Jr., *Moving Up*. New York: Morrow (1985), p. 77.
P. 112	"loyal to you." "Resurrecting Corporate Loyalty," *Fortune* (12/9/85), p. 207.
P. 112	"driveway or intersection." Richard Thain, *Think Twice Before You Accept That Job*. Homewood, Ill.: Dow Jones–Irwin (1986), p. 62, 154.
P. 114	"nice to me." Personal interview (1/86).
P. 115	"going to be there." Jeremy Mains, "Companies That Float From Owner to Owner," *Fortune* (4/28/86), p. 40.
P. 115	"nowhere else to go." "Job Loyalty: Not the Virtue It Seems," *NYT* (3/3/85), p. D1.
P. 116	Psychologists Salvatore Maddi and Suzanne Kobasa's book is *The Hardy Executive: Health Under Stress*. Homewood, Ill.: Dow Jones–Irwin (1984).
P. 116	"inner sense of mastery." Daniel Goleman, "Feeling of Control Viewed as Central in Mental Health," *NYT* (9/7/86), p. C11.
P. 117	"in the arts." Richard J. Thain, op. cit., pp. 33, 35.
P. 117	"[for] surrogate families." Jane Gross, "No More 9 to 5," *NYT*, The World of New York, (11/9/86), p. 46.
P. 118	"what it's all about." Personal interview (5/86).

CHAPTER 5

P. 120	"on the desert air." Richard Thain, op. cit., p. 153.
P. 121	likes his current employer. Follow-up interview (9/85).
P. 121	comparable employment elsewhere. Follow-up interviews (10/85; 1/87).
P. 123	"friends and associates." Carol Hymowitz, "More Executives Finding Changes in Traditional Corporate Ladder . . ." *WSJ* (11/14/86), p. 23.

P. 123	"too long to act." Edward F. Mrkvicka, Jr., op. cit., p. 140.
P. 124	"they don't bite." Personal interview (6/85).
P. 125	"with that particular attitude." Remarks at "Is Company Loyalty Going Out of Style?" Panel chaired by Paul Hirsch at the University of Chicago Graduate School of Business Management Conference (3/85).
P. 126	"you change jobs." Lynn Emmerman, "Middle-Aged Bosses Becoming Obsolete," *Chicago Tribune* (8/10/86), p. 6.
P. 127	"how to do that." Personal interview (7/85).
P. 128	"skills very broad." Personal interview (2/86).
P. 131	Mrkvicka, op. cit.
P. 132	"salary and rot?" Personal interview (3/86).
P. 134	"would get otherwise." Ibid.
P. 139	"teach to be princes." Myron Magnet, op. cit., p. 46.
P. 140	"with the deal itself." Ibid., pp. 45, 46.
P. 142	11-point list. From John L. Handy, "How to Face Being Taken Over," *Harvard Business Review* (November–December 1969), pp. 44–46.
P. 142	"didn't need me." In "Holding On in a Takeover," *BW* (9/27/82), p. 118.
P. 143	Robert Levering, Milton Moskowitz, and Michael Katz, *The 100 Best Companies to Work For in America.* Addison-Wesley: Reading, Mass. (1984).
P. 144	"their homework more." Amanda Bennett, "Middle Managers Face Job Squeeze as Cutbacks and Caution Spread," *WSJ* (4/25/86), p. 19.
P. 150	"wasted in restructuring." Rudolph Dew, personal interview (8/85).
P. 150	"laying off the 'good guys'." In Perry Pascarella, "When Change Means Saying You're Fired," *Industry Week* (7/7/86), pp. 47–48.
P. 153	"waste your time." In "The End of Corporate Loyalty?", op. cit., p. 48.
P. 154	"in the marketplace." Personal interview (11/85).

CHAPTER 6

P. 159 "where we are headed." Alex Taylor III, "What the Sober Spenders Will Buy," *Fortune* (2/2/87), p. 37.

P. 162 "[provide lifetime employment]." Peter Nulty, "How Managers Will Manage," *Fortune* (2/2/87), p. 47.

P. 162 "in large companies." Ibid., p. 50.

P. 162 "to a better job." "The End of Corporate Loyalty?", op. cit., p. 48.

P. 164 "loses its advantage." Pamela Sherrod, "50-plus looking good to employers," *Chicago Tribune* (11/11/85), section 4, p. 10.

P. 165 "than sheer energy." Ibid.

P. 165 "the higher ages." Richard Thain, op. cit., p. 83.

P. 168 Victor Kiam, *Going for It! How to Succeed as an Entrepreneur.* New York: Morrow (1986).

P. 169 "me a favor." Jean Ogden Freseman, "Starting Over," *Venture* (December 1985), p. 58.

P. 170 "make asinine mistakes." In "The Entrepreneurial Mystique," *Inc.* (10/85), p. 38.

Index